You Never Know What You Have… Till You Give It Away

and other important lessons in leadership

by Brian C. Stiller

Other books by Brian C. Stiller:
When Life Hurts, HarperCollins
What Happens When I Die? HarperCollins
Jesus and Caesar: Christians in the Public Square, Castle Quay Books
Preaching Parables to Postmoderns, Augsburg Fortress Publishers

YOU NEVER KNOW WHAT YOU HAVE *TILL YOU GIVE IT AWAY*

And Other Important Lessons in Leadership

BRIAN C. STILLER

You Never Know What You Have Till You Give it Away: and other important lessons in leadership

Printed in Canada
International Standard Book Number: 978-1-894860-44-4

Published by:
Castle Quay Books
1307 Wharf Street, Pickering, Ontario, L1W 1A5
Tel: (416) 573-3249
E-mail: info@castlequaybooks.com
www.castlequaybooks.com

Copy edited by Janet Dimond
Proofread by Marina Hofman
Cover design by THINKHOUSE COMMUNICATION DESIGN
Printed at Essence Publishing, Belleville, Ontario

Library and Archives Canada Cataloguing in Publication

Stiller, Brian C

You never know what you have : till you give it away / Brian C. Stiller.

Includes bibliographical references.
ISBN 978-1-894860-44-4

1. Leadership. I. Title.

HM1261.S75 2010 303.3'4 C2010-905066-5

Table of Contents

Dedication

To the many members of boards I have had the privilege to serve, for your wisdom and grace in letting me learn how to lead, giving me space and opportunities to both fail and succeed.

Introduction

These editorials began with the writing of the *Issachar Notes* online. A Jewish chronicler noted this about a Hebrew tribe King David had recruited in rebuilding Israel: *The sons of the tribe of Issachar had an understanding of the times and knew what Israel should do* (see 1 Chronicles 12:32).

This description defined my contribution in ministry. I early had an interest in how social and political dynamics shape faith and witness. While serving with Youth for Christ this interest grew, but found its real vocational opportunity in serving with which was, at first, a small and unorganized association—the Evangelical Fellowship of Canada.

As the topic of leadership—a relatively new discipline—only emerged in the late 1980s, I was interested but could find few substantive books. Later as president of Tyndale, I was encouraged by the writings of friend and spiritual mentor, Norm Allen, to reflect on leadership and its implications. I developed a habit of noting comments on leading and from that began to editorialize on the Web. I tried to point out the tough side of leading from those war stories we all have. Soon, readers gave feedback.

None of us in leadership are immune to weakness, self-doubt and making mistakes. We're human, and sometimes we get so caught up in our anxieties that we lose our focus. Keep these principles in mind:

- Jesus wants what others ignore.
- He blesses what others underestimate.
- Few give—most take.
- Take the gifts you've been given and give them away.

These are just the beginning of several lessons I've learned in my journey through leadership. How rich have been the insights and lessons given from so many.

For most of these editorials, Ruth Whitt carefully scrutinized language, grammar and syntax. My style was the subject of many conversations, but in the end she allowed pass this another of my idiosyncrasies. Janet Dimond has, with an amazing eye for content and selection, ordered and edited this final version, for which I'm so grateful.

I'm thankful for the opportunity to learn this trade of leading. Understanding our times, and from that developing strategies, is what we as leaders need to do.

September 2010

You Never Know What You Have

Jesus Wants What Others Ignore

Moses didn't know what he had—until he gave it away.
He learned this rather dramatically:

"What's in your hand?"
"Not much, Lord. A working shepherd's staff."
"Throw it down." (It turns into a snake.)
"Wow. How did you do that?"

Most leaders have little idea what they have. The times we're filled with our self-importance usually end up in failure and embarrassment.

The story-classic is Jesus feeding the 5,000. His disciples downplayed any expectation that people could be fed. Why, even the small boy's lunch they found wouldn't give a few a meagre bites. Here the Creation story is played out. All sophistication of modern farming, the very best of entrepreneurial ingenuity, is reduced to the three elements of this story.

First, Jesus wants what others ignore.

Dr. Christiaan Barnard of South Africa was successful in performing heart transplants in the late 1960s and early 1970s, but within days all of his patients died. The new hearts were seen as foreign and were rejected by the body. At about the same time, scientists in Switzerland working to discover new antibiotics to fight infection found that fungi grown in soil samples from Norway and Wisconsin produced an opposite expected result. Instead of being useful fighting infection, they caused the host to be *more* vulnerable to infection by shutting down the immune system.

As the chief scientist was about to shut down this particular research, Jean-François Borel, remembering Barnard's problem, asked if he could continue the project. He did, and in a short time cyclosporine was developed, which revolutionized the world of medicine, and made successful organ transplants possible.

What's in your hand? Do you feel unappreciated, overlooked, ignored? Do you feel a sense of failure, unable to find any life of significance? What others ignore, Jesus wants. Leave to Him what it truly is worth. You never know what you have till you give it away.

Prayer—

My hunch, Lord, is that what I have isn't worth a whole lot. In fact, most others don't even know I have it. However, I've decided: I'll give you what I have. How and where You use it is now up to You. Help me to be faithful in giving every day what has come my way. Amen

Jesus Blesses What Others Underestimate

Look over a crowd of teenagers, some rowdy, others withdrawn, and the majority buzzed by the noisy ones. Try to figure out who will influence significant change in the world. You can't.

Flip through your high school yearbook and read the quotes and aspirations. If you've attended a reunion, did you predict all those years ago who would step out onto a stage and shape their part of the world? Months after a sports team has spent millions on drafting and trading players, they bemoan those they missed who excelled elsewhere and those they recruited who disappointed. Every player isn't a Wayne Gretzky. There's no way to predict. Most often we underestimate others and ourselves. There are obvious ingredients of intellect and sometimes talent. What's more difficult to see is heart. Like the bumblebee. Engineering-wise, it can't fly. But it does anyhow.

Embedded in the fish and bread were the ingredients to make more. The disciples didn't see that. And neither did the crowd. They wanted to eat, and the disciples knew they had a disaster on their hands if they didn't do something soon. Money and buying food was their option. A young boy, prized by his mother and equipped to handle the day, didn't register with the disciples. In the boy's hands was the answer.

Underestimated.

The hometown folk wondered about Jesus, the boy who grew up with their sons. "Why, isn't he Joseph's son?" someone remarked. Ordinary. Unremarkable. Further, how could anyone they knew this well be significant? How dare He!

Floating around in conversations, I hear seemingly wise comments: "You know, we just don't have leaders like we used to." And people nod their heads and mumble foolish affirmations. It's always been like that. We see leaders in hindsight. Those who lead now are ordinary and like us. We would wish greatness, charismatic jumping-buildings-in-a-single-leap. If that's the kind of leader you have, they're probably better at grandstanding than leading.

Leaders emerge from among us. They're common. No signs hanging above their doors announcing their gift to lead. It's what we find when we give the underestimated the opportunity to open their hands and offer up their apparently meagre provisions. Goliath scorned scrawny David. Nazareth underestimated Jesus. Felix, the Roman governor, didn't realize he was up against the great first-century mind of Paul of Tarsus.

Most will underestimate you. But don't underestimate yourself. Allow the inner resilience of faith to hold on to the gifting that's yours by creation and nurture, ever willing in His time to take your modest offerings and multiply them beyond what you ever expected.

Prayer—

Lord, they seem so insignificant. There are times I feel like the runt in the litter. Then I remember I'm Yours, and Your gifting is a gift I'm not to keep hidden, by either selfish interest or insecurity. So here it is. Surprise them, Lord, and may You be praised in the doing. Amen.

Few Give–Most Take

There are two kinds of people in the world—givers and takers. And all of us are somewhere in-between.

What occurs to most as they set out for the day, especially those who work outside the home?

Will I today find in my work and relationships the money I need to live, the feelings I require for well-being, and a sufficiently pleasant environment to get on with life?

How often in the past seven days have your starting moments been framed by "How many ways can I give today?" This isn't meant to induce guilt, but rather to alert us to the uncommonness of the intention to give. Giving isn't an automatic impulse. Taking is.

Even in the feeding of the 5,000 story, only one gave. The boy. He gave up what was his. Was there a promise he would even get a morsel to eat? Jesus took from him. The disciples took from Jesus. The people took from the disciples. Then the disciples took back from the people what was left over. Out of over 5,000, only one gave.

I earlier noted the Creation story is played out in this moment. Farmers, investors and parents know it well. You begin with the essential elements. These are sown, invested, ploughed underground. They die. Well not quite, but it sure looks like it.

Only as it's given away can it multiply. That one seed by creation is destined to become many—but only when given away. If hoarded, it sits in the granary. I know many who in generosity give and give and give. Their joy and pleasure in giving is unbounded. Then I meet those bound up in fear of giving. For them, it's hard. The power and combined joy of those who live with generosity releases them, so that in the giving, their open hands are able to receive more.

But beware. There are those who imply that by giving, we'll become rich. Their hucksterism corrodes the beauty of this Creation principle.

Giving is not to get. You get in your giving, but if that's your motive, the very spirit of the Jesus we follow is violated and corrupted.

Leaders, we're to give, as is anyone out of their gifting. Leaders have a special need, for it falls in part to us to provide a flow of life, energy and hope as conduits of His grace. This necessitates learning how to give. It's a discipline. It's learned. In doing it—especially in times when it threatens our well-being—it becomes natural, and in time becomes the first impulse, the dominant instinct.

Prayer—

Source of life, Giver of all that's good, help me break free from a spirit of wanting others to give me today those elements of life I want, need or request. And instead incline my heart and train my mouth to ever give. Amen.

Who Was Agnes Gonxha Bojaxhiu?

At age 18, she knew her life would be different. At 40, she founded the Missionaries of Charity. For another 20 years, she worked in obscurity. We know her as Mother Teresa.

No one in our generation defined Christian love as did Mother Teresa. Mention her name and images of care and compassion surface. I hadn't known her tough oversight of the worldwide ministry. A TV documentary showed her reviewing a new centre on the US west coast. With a quick glance at the furnishings, she ordered them removed and replaced with more modest ones. To romanticize her is to miss what she was about.

What we may also overlook are the years she spent in drudgery and obscurity before her name and work spread across the media. The model of service that had its larger impact years later was refined in those obscure years. That's not to say that what we do in obscurity will inevitably find its way to a Nobel Prize. Our work may not surface for years, and possibly not ever. William Carey's 40 years of missionary labour with one convert was not the measurement of his calling or effectiveness. That came decades later.

Paul maps out the process: "Suffering produces perseverance; perseverance, character; and character hope," (Romans 5:3,4). There's a line each leader follows, like it or not. Farmers will tell you. The cold spring day and the harsh north wind remind them that unless the seed is planted, there will be no harvest. The obscure seed, germinating and growing oh so slowly, is the only way the multiple effect takes place.

Glamour, power and money seem to be an underlying measurement of some religious communities. Do you watch some of the high-flying media artists do their biblical act and wonder how they seem so successful, while you grind out in the obscure and small places? It seems so unfair.

Mother Teresa modelled the Lord Jesus. That she became world-famous is counterintuitive. What matters is that she lived out the Gospel. She died the same day as Princess Diana. A columnist said, "Princess Di touched the poor; Mother Teresa took them home."

Let the spin masters do their work with those they choose, but live out His calling and life, and may that be your reward.

Prayer—

God of Eternity, the One who is in no hurry in working out Your purposes, keep me from thinking that if there's no apparent success this week or year, all is lost. The sowing and reaping cycle is Your design, and for good reason. This day, in my thinking, praying and managing, may the rhythm of Your good Creation be replicated. Amen.

Blooming Where Planted

"Like a lot of beautiful things, tulips inspire malfeasance, and they take a lot of work to maintain. Careless people pick them. Mice, rats, voles, skunks, squirrels and deer eat them. Even in Holland, they need a lot of human intervention to thrive because they'd rather be on a rocky mountainside in Turkey, where they come from."

—*Constance Casey*

Leading, like growing tulips, isn't easy. Leaders start out with a particular DNA, a journey that inevitably requires a kind of death. This is like Jesus' line: "Unless a seedling falls into the ground and dies, it doesn't reproduce or grow—followed then by sprouts overcoming the resistant soil, pushing into the daylight, drawing in nutrients," (John 12:24).

Recall the minister who stopped by his parishioner's farm, and, looking over the meticulously cared-for field, commented, "Isn't God's Creation beautiful?"

"Yeah, I suppose," the farmer grunted, "but you should've seen it when He had it all to himself."

The gifting of God is not automatic. We've all seen tragic failures of those so gifted, yet by poor choices, crippling life experiences or laziness, fritter away life, leaving the bulb carelessly tossed aside in a corner of the garden. To those who have much, much is required. My sense is it'll sound rather hollow as we enter the Kingdom and, when asked for His return on investment, mutter, "Well, I was persecuted." "I ran out of energy." "I felt insecure." "I couldn't make up my mind." "No one would listen." Blooming calls for daily, conscious choices.

Prayer—

Tulip Maker, Fashioner of the *imago Dei*, this Creation is of Your doing. Help me see what too is of my doing so in the course of this day,

I'll not let the wish of the bulb to return to Turkey override the need to bloom where planted. Amen.

Grace Costs

"Cheap grace is the preaching of forgiveness without requiring repentance, baptism without church discipline, communion without confessional, absolution without personal confession. Cheap grace is grace without discipleship, grace without the cross, grace without Jesus Christ—living and incarnate."

—*Dietrich Bonhoeffer*

Walter Wangerin Jr., in his marvellous story-bible of the New Testament—*Jesus: A Novel*—describes what Mary sees when a woman dropped in her coins at the temple:

> *A very old woman had just pulled herself up to her feet. She began to shuffle through the Court of the Women in a direction somewhat slant of us. She pressed a begging bowl in both hands against her stomach. Soon, though she took desperately small steps, we knew her direction, if not her mind: she was moving toward the treasury just to the right of us. As she crept by, I saw her in profile: a long translucent nose; eyelids loose, the low rims sagging from their eyeballs, her mouth working like a Pharisee at prayer. When she reached the treasury, she brought forth the begging bowl and turned it slowly over the bell-like mouth, and two tiny bits of metal fell from the bowl into the bronze.*
>
> *We could hear nothing of the fall.*
>
> "*Judas, my brother, my bright disciples,*" *Jesus said.* "*Know the difference. Live by it: those rich men who contributed wonderful sums to the temple were contributing something of their surplus. It never touched their need. But this woman who gave two copper mites—she has given more than ten such notables combined. For she gave all she had. It was everything she had to live on.*"

Bonhoeffer's famous line about cheap grace warns us against assuming that life in Christ costs us nothing. Grace is a rich theological idea birthed in God's giving to us what we don't deserve. In offering grace at mealtime, we make known we're receiving from His hand what we don't deserve.

There are two implications. On the giving side, grace is grace when it costs us. On the receiving side, we cheapen it when we let others assume it requires no sacrificial response. Our eyes could do with a Jesus-clarity.

Prayer—

My loving and truth-revealing Jesus, stressed by relentless requirements to balance budgets, I need to know, as well as my leader-friends, how You assess and judge our service. Keep me from determining my significance as a leader by my association with people of power. Help me, God of Stewardship, to know that grace in leadership is costly, and give me insight to see that those who give out of their need and not of their surplus truly understand sacrificial giving. Amen.

Risk Is What We Practise

"Don't expect others to take greater risks or make greater sacrifices than you have."

—*Andy Stanley*

How easy it is for us to slip behind the larger vision, pressing others to join in, all the while keeping our powder dry. My argument goes this way: "I'm spending my energy in getting the idea going. That's my contribution." And in matters of giving, I slip into this rationalization: "I live on a modest salary, and because I get less than I might receive elsewhere, the difference is my gift."

One day, while meeting with Henry Wildeboer, a friend and coach, he asked bluntly, "Brian, what are you giving to the campaign?" His reference was to a very large capital campaign—for us—of $58 million. To many of whom I've asked to give major gifts, I've said, "If we don't think in terms larger than we've ever thought before, we simply won't achieve this goal."

So when Henry asked, I told him of our commitment—the largest we'd ever made. His abrupt question was, "Is that a relatively easy gift or is it real sacrifice?" Here the Spirit bumped hard against my rationalization. In the end, Lily and I pushed ourselves beyond what was seemingly feasible. I knew that unless the sacrifice was a stretching of our faith, how could I ask others to do the same?

Missionary statesman Oswald J. Smith taught his church to give on a Faith Promise plan. It was simple, but profoundly biblical. Beyond one's normal tithe, at a particular moment in the year, he encouraged people to pledge an amount to give in the next 12 months beyond what they in the normal course of living could do. The *promise* is made by *faith*, meaning the amount is predicated on the Lord helping me fulfill the promise. I know that by ordinary means I can't, so I must rely on the Lord by faith. The income needed to meet the pledge will come from a variety of sources: Aunt Amy leaves a bequest; I find I can get on with less; a new job comes along with added income; I figure out a creative way to raise funds. The list goes on.

That simple principle has pressed us to give in new and deeply satisfying ways, for it becomes a partnership by faith—and by that we're transformed.

Prayer—

Father, Owner of the cattle scattered across the hills of this country, may the risk of faith we ask others to exercise not be lost on us. For we know the joy of obedience is found in pushing ourselves in faith beyond what we can do ourselves. Amen.

The Art of Leading

Is Meek Weak?

"In the *Atlantic Monthly*, Mary Karr relates that her friend, a Franciscan nun, says that to grasp the meaning of meek, we should 'picture a great stallion at full gallop...At its master's voice—[it] seizes up to a stunned but instant halt.'"

—Harold Myra

I've never much liked the word "meek." The King James Version uses it to describe Moses, but it sounds too much like "weak" to me. This analogy reverses the image. Moses was anything but weak. Having to manage 12 primitive tribes, weakness wasn't what he needed to control their collective egos, attitudes and self-righteousness. He had to be tough (Numbers 12:2-4).

Leaders now and then have no choice but to bite down on the bit and move forward. For some, it may suit your personality. If not, there are times difficult choices must be made and that falls to the leader.

When authority pulls on the reins, whispers or shouts, "Whoa!" meekness respects authority, overriding my determination to keep moving, be that authority God, my board or my supervisor. I may shake my mane and flare my nostrils, but obey I will.

Meek is not weak. Meekness implies power, strength and fortitude. I'm impressed when the most powerful horse in the herd responds immediately to its master's whistle or pulls on the bit. The stronger, the more remarkable response to authority.

Meekness is a word reserved for the "Moses" of the world. Samson, with enormous physical strength, was weak, not meek. It took the pulverizing pull of load-bearing columns, ending in his death, for his life to have impact. His inability to respond to the "bit" of the Lord made him weak in the arms of his lover.

Moses, while strong willed, impatient and forced to learn the hard way, did come to understand that when God pulled on the reins, to be strong was to be meek, and meekness is saying "yes" to the One who holds the reins.

Prayer—

Holder of the Reins, in times when I think mine is the only way, may the internal tug of my heart and the external discipline of my work develop a capacity to respond to authorities You've put in my life. May meekness be a hallmark of strength. Amen.

Time to Rattle the Cage?

"We all snickered at some writers who viewed Dad as a grand strategist who intuitively developed complex plans and implemented them with precision. Dad thrived on change, and no decision was ever sacred."

—*Jim Walton, writing about his father Sam Walton, founder of Walmart*

Creators of large enterprises most often stumble into success. Canadian humourist Stephen Leacock noted, "I am a great believer in luck, and I find the harder I work, the more I have of it."

Leadership is made up of a complex array of skills, intuitive understandings, personal qualities, opportunities and timing with no set or combination true for all. Those who are enormously successful in one generation or location may not have been so successful had they been born in another time or place.

Walton thrived on change. For some, that's scary. American philosopher William Durant said, in effect, it's the tragedy of things spiritual that we languish if disorganized, and yet we're destroyed by the material means of our organization.

Organizations get stuck in their ways. Leaders from time to time need to rattle cages—upsetting the status quo, pressing the organization into change, sometimes for the sake of change itself. Within the trauma and unsettledness of change, ideas emerge, people's talents unfold and external realities become opportunities—not threats.

Religious organizations are also resistant to change. It's strange, isn't it, since the Gospel is built on leaving comforts of the present and moving into unknown and unpredictable places. For many, however, the Spirit—the Cloud, the Fire—has already moved on and they're still camped in their present comfort zone. Conservative theology can by its nature breed organizational conservatism—reluctance to change.

If your style is not to ruffle feathers, but to comfort the anxious and smooth out the walkway, it may be time for you to leave and give place to a dust-disturber. Or take a risk, and press your people or congregation into a process by which they choose to take a risk on change.

Prayer—

Great Spirit of God who led Abraham from his home, who disturbed Moses to upset Your people, who rankled the tedious conventions of the Pharisees to raise up Paul to lead, in this day and place, may we discover the joy of faith and trust as we thrive on those opportunities of change that serve Your great purposes. Amen.

The Fallacy of Certainty

"The opposite of faith is not doubt but certainty."

—*Anne Lamont*

It's counterintuitive. To have faith, shouldn't I be certain? It's here that logic betrays the point. Shouldn't people of faith be certain of what they do, where they lead, where or what they plant? And isn't fear the opposite? And by extension, isn't to be fearful to be faithless?

Definitions matter. Webster's New World Dictionary has five for "faith." But here our sloppy, multiuse of "faith" serves us poorly. It can mean anything from "What's your religion?" to unquestioning belief.

The Scriptures have a particular way of shaping its meaning. Faith in God is to so trust in Him that if He fails, we're doomed. We put all our eggs into one basket. There's no sidestepping. Christians put their lives, their totality, into trusting that who He claims to be and what He promises to be are true. But what if it isn't? What if He isn't? Then we've got nowhere to turn. If God doesn't show up, we're sunk.

If I'm certain, I don't need to exercise faith. Frankly, much of what we do could be done by someone who doesn't believe in God.

Faith, worn thin by careless verbiage and trite claims, loses its wonder and therefore, power. Recall Joshua, bumping up against the Jordan, pushed by tired Israelites who wanted access to the Promised Land. "What am I to do?" he asks. "When the feet of the priests touch the water, I'll stop it," the Lord replies. Joshua might have said, "Interesting. But I have another idea. You stop the water and then we'll walk across." (See Joshua 3.)

Faith is what we do, not what we believe. It's being vulnerable to trust. It means we proceed without Plan B. Biblical stories are filled with leaders who practised faith. Too often I say, "I'm living by faith," but just in case, I build a bridge or two. Certainty is good. Faith is quite different. In fact, it's the opposite. It's to operate in a zone that casts us beyond our capabilities and capacities.

Prayer—

The Great You who called Abraham to leave the Silicon Valley of his day, and by faith go where he had no idea, may we know the fright and joy of that faith walk. May no silliness or grandstanding mar Your grand call to authentic faith. Instead, dear Lord, help break the demanding need for certainty as by faith we walk to the water's edge. Amen.

What's Wrong with Blue Footballs?

"Real football players don't play with blue footballs."

—B. Pascal

"Here, take one of these," said Phil Kay, director of admissions and marketing at Tyndale, as he threw me a couple of small, soft blue footballs. "High school kids love these. We throw them out to students during recruitment assemblies. Your grandsons will love them." That night, our daughter, her husband and two boys—five and two at the time—were at our home for supper. "Brycen, after supper, you and I can play football. Here's one I brought just for you," I said as I threw him the small, soft blue football. What fun we had.

The next evening as we talked by phone, I said, "Brycen, that was great last night playing football. Let's do it again." Silence.

Finally, "Papa, next time I'll bring my brown football. Okay?"

"Sure. But why a brown football?" I asked.

"Papa, real football players don't play with blue footballs."

When does instinct kick in? I get a little tired of leadership books stocked with "should," "ought" or "must." Who says I "should," I "ought," I "must"? The fact is that each of us as leaders brings to our calling and assignment a set of human characteristics, personality traits and learned patterns different from others.

Notwithstanding the importance of learning from others—lectures, books or on the job—there is within each of us inherent knowledge. While the nature/nurture debate continues to draw no definitive conclusions, I opt for the importance of learning to lead with intuition.

Creation is marvellous and complex. From it we draw from the reservoir of the *imago Dei*. Be reluctant to allow self-doubt to keep you from mining rich veins from which the raw stuff of life is forged.

If your instinct is that blue footballs aren't for you, I'd say trust your hunch.

Prayer—

Loving Father, at times I'm nervous to trust what I intuitively feel or what I see at first glance. I've been so wrong before. Yet help me to know that Your work began in Creation and continues by what Your Spirit is doing in and around me today. Being right 100 per cent of the time is not my goal. Obedience is. In this search for doing good as a leader, help me trust what You've made and continue to make in this ever-learning calling of faith. Amen.

Shaping the Times

"He was among the foremost of those who fixed the character of his times."

Walk into Westminster Abbey and you'll see on William Wilberforce's tomb this epitaph:

> *In an age and country fertile in great and good men, he was among the foremost of those who fixed the character of his times.*
>
> *Because to the high and various talents, to warm benevolence and to universal candour, he added the abiding eloquence of a Christian life.*

On July 26, 1833, shortly before he died, the British House of Commons passed the Slavery Abolition Bill—the bill he had worked most of his life to see passed.

I know we must be careful not to become what we aren't and what the times don't call for, but I'm struck by the power of the idea: *He was among the foremost of those who fixed the character of his times.* We all "fix" the character of our times, be it with our children, grandchildren, business associates or neighbours. For most of us, what we fix is not nation shaping as with Wilberforce, but we do influence, whether we intend to or not.

In describing King David, the Apostle Paul in a message to the Jewish community gives a simple, seemingly throw-away line: "For when David had served God's purpose in his own generation, he fell asleep" (Acts 13:36).

You and I, like King David or William Wilberforce, have a purpose, and it is to influence and shape our environment and assumptions.

Prayer—

Father of Life and Light, by Your indwelling Spirit, help me to be conscious of the "fixing" my life affects this day, and by Your love and grace may the voice others hear too have an "eloquence of a Christian life." Amen.

God Talks?

A popular joke goes like this:

"Our rabbi talks to God every Saturday."
"What makes you think so?"
"The rabbi told us himself."
"What if the rabbi lies?"
"Don't be ridiculous. God wouldn't talk to a liar every Saturday."

Even within this convoluted logic, we agree that God speaks to us. Abraham heard God's voice and moved from the leading-edge culture of his day to a place beyond what was familiar. My father, raised in a Swedish immigrant family on the Canadian Prairies, told me that one day while ploughing, he heard a clear and unambiguous voice: "Son, work in my vineyard today."

If someone else had been standing where Abraham or my father were, would they have heard it too? Did my father hear an audible voice? Or was it an impression, a collection of sayings heard in another place and time? I don't know.

One day, in a critical moment in my ministry, at the lowest point of institutional existence, my wife—knowing little of the issues at hand—pointed to a marvellous campus we were passing and said, "Brian, some day the Lord will give that to you." I felt a chill. The Lord had spoken.

Most times, a word from God comes from a biblical text, or is carried in a book, saying or prayer. It creates impressions that over time are confirmed by other words or events that lead us to say, "I believe the Lord has spoken."

We know the excesses, the disasters, and outright manipulation that such assertions can bring. However, that shouldn't keep us from listening. Those He calls to steward resources and move forward a vision need to hear His voice.

Some nine years later, we owned the campus.

Prayer—

Wise God and Spirit-Counsellor, at times I'm too clever by half. Surrounded by the commotion of strategic moves and well-devised plans, too often I hear only chattering voices. I confess that listening has never been my strength. A talker is what I am. Words are my currency. Keep me from configuring my ideas into what I claim are Your words. Give me ears to hear and recognize Your voice. And if I don't, bring a priest like the Old Testament Eli into my life, so, as with Samuel, I'll know when You speak. Amen.

The Bigger Picture

"Throw your nets on the other side."

—*Jesus*

What in the world does a carpenter know about fishing? That may have been Peter's question when he heard Jesus call out across the water in John 21:6.

An outsider can be a pain in the neck. Like the time I was struggling to uncouple a barbecue. A woman observing asked, "Brian, why not turn it the other way?" Two good reasons to ignore her: 1. You *always* turn a nut to the left to get it off, and 2. Well, forgive my assumption that things mechanical are usually best handled by a male.

What's the issue? Trapped in the tactics of the moment, we work harder. Not unlike the English-speaking tourist in India who, when seemingly unable to make himself understood, spoke louder.

It takes someone else to see what we don't. It's perspective. A coach can help. Asking another what they see that you don't is freeing. It helps me remember that I see only partially. Another's view will help broaden mine.

Not surprisingly, many of us as leaders trip over this. Headstrong, we clearly see the way ahead and have come to trust our instincts. Vision not only gives the contours of the plan, it paints in the details. When someone seems to be poking their objections in the spokes of our wheels, we push them aside, or at best ignore them and move on.

There are times when others know best. For a fisherman of Peter's personality to take instruction from a land-locked carpenter would be worthy of a film script. The dynamics would be humorous—until the application is made to me.

So after a frustrating moment of embarrassed failure, I followed the woman's advice—and it worked.

Prayer—

Lord Jesus, Carpenter, Fisher, Counsellor, when I'm fixated on one side of the boat, keep me from insisting to fish my way. Instead, shake my self-confidence enough so that I know that others can help me see what I don't. Amen.

Ignoring Flies

"Sometimes if a racehorse pays too much attention to a horsefly, it makes the fly too important. Some people's only taste of success is the bite they take out of someone whom they perceive is doing more than they are."

Fred Smith, speaking of Billy Graham's critics
—as told by Harold Myra

Oh, the sting of unfair criticism. Even when fair, it hurts. But when undeserved? Thin-skinned, I replay my tapes of defence, edited and refined through multiple playings. Leadership and criticism go together.

When criticism is deserved, respond. Ask for forgiveness. In working with young people, I'd advise them, "When you blow it, ask your parents or teachers to forgive you. What else can they do?"

Correct it, whatever it is. Do something about it.

But when criticism is unfair, undeserved or inaccurate, then what? Smith warns not to give it more credence than it deserves. His picture is compelling—a horse coming down the last quarter mile, fussing about a fly!

Myra's book on Graham provides many good examples of his focus on the important. I saw the same. In 1995, I co-chaired his five-day Toronto mission. Shortly after arriving in the city and before the meetings began, he fell ill and was hospitalized.

Two evenings later Lily and I arrived home. On our answering machine was a message from him. An issue had arisen—one of personal complexity for him. He didn't want it to affect the work of the Spirit and the years of planning. He wanted me to know of his excitement over the coming meetings, and his sorrow over unwise and misplaced conversations of others. There he was, lying in a hospital bed, unable to speak at the first of three evenings at the Toronto SkyDome. He refused to allow the matter to set aside the "race." The "fly" didn't get in the way.

Prayer—

Lord Jesus, even though we know personal criticism is inevitable, this day and week let grace rise in our hearts. May we be gracious to face our failings. May we also find discipline in our minds and plans to not let fair and unfair criticism detract from the important roles we're called by You to fill. Amen.

Leading with Vision

First, Walk

"If you have raced with men on foot and they have worn you out, how can you compete with horses? If you stumble in safe country, how will you manage in the thickets by the Jordan?"

—*Jeremiah 12:5*

Wishing I knew years ago what I know today is a waste of time. Life's lessons come in the course of living. I'm wrong to assume I would've benefited if only someone had told me earlier. Experience is central to God's pedagogy. There are two ingredients in Jeremiah's picture: begin at the beginning. Vision and drive notwithstanding, there's only one way to learn: *we walk before we run.* We first learn to compete with our own kind before we take on horses. We walk on smooth land before we take on rough terrain.

For those of you at the beginning of vocational leadership, there's something wonderful about your confidence and know-it-all attitude. Don't apologize for it. However, there's no shortcut to the majors. To contribute, you'll put in your time, learning how to run in the race of beginners.

For those closer to the end, we had no other way to learn than to practise, and through the rough and tumble classroom of doing, learn. For those in mid- or late vocation, the failures we see in the rear-view mirror are troubling. However, we could only learn by stumbling. Navigating is a learned skill. Don't allow regrets to steal from you the lessons and wisdom that accumulate through life. They're yours—a treasure.

Robert Clinton, in *The Making of a Leader*, breaks up life and ministry experience into six phases. Phase five is "convergence," a time in which there's a match of gift-mix, experience, temperament and opportunity. "In convergence, being and spiritual authority form the true power for mature ministry." It's by the converging of experience, giftings and opportunities we're able to take on the more difficult callings.

Prayer—

Lord, as I examine issues needing insight, the relationships needing caring, and the unknowns needing Your leading, help me to trust that the life experiences of the past and the constant leading of Your Spirit will connect at the right time and place for Your Kingdom and glory. Amen.

Seeing Beyond

"If you want to build a ship, don't drum up the men to gather wood, divide the work, and give orders. Instead, teach them to yearn for the vast and endless sea."

—*Antoine de Saint-Exupéry*

A visitor standing at the building site of St. Peter's Basilica turned to a worker sweeping up the construction debris of the day and asked, "And what are you doing?" The sweeper replied, "Building a great temple for God." There was brilliance somewhere in that community of workers. Some manager was smart enough to draw everyone from Michelangelo to the sweeper into a vision.

Ministry is done amidst the grind of daily tasks. For sure, "the devil's in the details." As much as we prefer bold vision and times of ministry success, we still have to roll out of bed in the morning, get to the office, school, church or mission, and go through what may seem to be drudgery. So how can we lift the eyes of our colleagues so that in building the great cathedral of God, they see their tasks as being more than sweepers?

Sir Francis Drake tried to recruit young men to go with him on an exploration. He told them of the marvels of their travel—pristine beaches, untold treasures and wealth beyond their imagination. He didn't expect that no one would join.

The next day, he reversed his approach. Warning them of fearful storms, possible loss of life at sea, terrifying natives and excruciating shortage of food and water, he ended with a promise that if they could endure these challenges, there would be an enormous reward at the end. A reversal of the day before, he was overwhelmed with applicants. Their imaginations were fired by challenges, rather than pleasure.

May those with whom we work—be it in the business office or in custodial services—say when asked, "What is your work?" respond, "I'm part of God's advance team in bringing in His Kingdom."

Prayer—

Jesus Christ, Lord and King, help me—along with Your disciples—lift up my eyes from the surrounding grunt work of ministry and vocation, and see beyond to the Kingdom that is now here and coming. May I be motivated today with an eye to Your promise, so that the joy of Your Kingdom come may resonate in every computer stroke, paper turned and word spoken. Amen.

What's Your Plan?

"If your vision is for a year, plant wheat.
If your vision is for ten years, plant trees.
If your vision is for a lifetime, plant people."

—*Chinese proverb*

Don't allow this proverb to impose guilt with its implication that short- and medium-term goals are inferior. True, without a long-term vision we muddle in the micro, fussing over arranging seats or lining up paper clips. Unless I can define in two minutes or less why what I'm doing now matters 20 years from now, I'm probably lost in the muddle.

With that as our backdrop, let's focus our attention on short- and medium-term goals. In my experience, this is where we drop the ball.

In North American football, excitement builds toward the end of a game, with two minutes left and the score close enough that if the losing team can score a touchdown in the remaining seconds, they'll win. Starting from deep in their end zone, the quarterback executes a play-by-play strategy that gradually moves them forward, and, with just seconds left, makes the final move that takes them into the end zone for victory.

The whole team had a lifetime vision for winning. It's the leader who executes short-term plans. With an eye on the clock and a strategic awareness of the opposing team, he deftly integrates his team's strengths to strike at their opponent's weaknesses.

Current leadership lingo is "vision." As valuable as that is, the usual faltering in executing strategies to meet vision is from a lack of knowledge around *What are we doing this month, week, day?* I know, because this is my weakness. I love talking vision, the big picture, seeing life from 33,000 feet. My language and thoughts are peppered with these metaphors.

I wish I had learned decades ago to insist on business plans. Not with a quick hour-or-two scribble of what I hope we'll do, but a logically and systematically organized plan that not only makes sense to others, it becomes a measurement against which what I do can actually be measured. It's no wonder to me why NGOs and not-for-profits flounder. We clearly see the bigger vision, but that's not usually our problem. We cover up laziness or a lack of professional competence with too much language, gushing over vision.

The next time anyone wows you with vision, ask to see their business plan. Fiery words are vital, but without careful planning, it may end up being just that.

Prayer—

God of Vision and ordered Creation, keep me as a leader within the discipline of enabling vision to be realized. May the prosaic and dull elements needed to bring about vision not be ignored. By Your Spirit, fan the fire, so that the life-energy required to make the vision a reality will be as deeply satisfying as describing the vision. Amen.

What's Your Mission?

"My mission is to ease pain and extend life."

—*Dr. Calvin R. Stiller*

Cal, my older brother and arguably one of the best-known medical scientists in Canada, pioneered organ transplants, and is at the forefront of medical advance and research in Canada and worldwide. I heard him give the above line at a dinner in his honour at the University of Western Ontario. All that he did—his life, training and discipline—could be reduced to that nine-word mission.

So what's yours? Setting aside specific goals for this month or year, the details of running your organization, the dull stuff of daily work—what's your life about? Can you state it in a few words?

1 Chronicles 12:32 has become my life verse. David, in rebuilding Israel, recruited tribes to help. One tribe was the Sons of Issachar (pronounced *Is-a-car*): they had an understanding of their times and knew what Israel should do. This text defined my call.

It became a framework for how I go about doing my work. First, know the setting—the context, perceptions, facts, realities, opportunities, needs and possible troubles. Then decipher a plan of action through the discipline of analysis.

I need the resistance that analysis imports. It holds me back. It refines my thinking. It keeps me from making too many mistakes.

My underlying motivation is to influence people to love and serve Christ. When I cross the divide, I want to hear, "Well done. Enter into your reward," (Matthew 25:14-30).

Even so, my life would be lived with much greater vigour if with clarity I could say each morning in the shower, "Today, Lord, I'll press forward in my life mission to..." (keep it under 20 words!).

Prayer—

Lord of Faith, The One Who Calls, help me with focus in my tomorrows. Some days I begin with clear purpose, while others I stumble into agendas. For too many meetings I arrive only because they're in my Blackberry. So Lord, Giver of Wisdom, may I be wise enough to know what really matters. Amen.

What's Your Trophy?

"If you don't have the Vince Lombardi trophy, everything else is a paperweight."

—*Coach Shanahan of the Denver Broncos*

Leaders are caught between using temporal trophies and eternal rewards as motivation. In for-profit endeavours, it seems easier and more sustainable to carrot employees with better compensation. Not-for-profits are more complex. However, we play the fool if we don't understand that temporality figures largely with employee satisfaction. The baseline of compensation should be fair and reasonable, both by salary and benefits. Our people live in the same world as for-profit employees.

Moving up the scale can be problematic. For mission agencies (let's call them M1) where staff raise their own support, setting wages and benefits engages a different dynamic. The employee, regardless of the level of compensation, has to raise that and more. Those funded by the money pool operate differently. Let's call them M2.

Increasingly, M2s are pushing their salary scale to better match their secular counterparts. This, on the surface, is good. Compensation fairly assessed presses agencies and organizations to lift their standards in all areas. For as compensation pushes an agency to do better in building its fiscal resources, there's generally initiative to improve its missional engagement.

But this still doesn't answer the issue of motivation and rewards. We know that within the context of fair and reasonable compensation, people are happy about their work for reasons other than money. Job satisfaction—all things being equal—comes mainly from sources other than salary scale and benefits.

The downside to this professionalism is what is the primary tug at our hearts? In life and ministry, what become the paperweights? What, for me—an employee—is my Lombardi trophy?

As president, my satisfaction came in ways not that different from any of our faculty or staff. But what drove me, day by day? When we met our goals, there was exhilaration. Celebration is essential to the human endeavour. But what else drives me?

Important as job descriptions and annual reviews are, go back to first principles. Trophies come from more than statistics; motivationally, I need to hear the Lord's voice more than accolades of peers or manager, and know that what I do ripples out onto eternity—that which is now and yet to come.

Prayer—

Lord of all, beyond trophies and human praise, let me feel the lift that comes from receiving the Lombardi trophy of Your giving. As much as I love to meet goals, overcome adversity and solve problems, may those successes then become paperweights compared to Your trophies. Amen.

What a Flap!

"As each goose flaps it wings, it creates an 'uplift' for the bird following. By flying in a V formation, the whole flock adds 71 per cent greater flying range than if each bird flew alone."

—*Robert McNeish*

I was in the middle of arguably the greatest challenge of my life. Never having an interest in buildings, there I was toward the end of my public leadership responsible for one of the largest fundraising projects—I was told—within a Roman Catholic or Protestant community in Canadian history.

As CEO, I knew I was responsible for bringing together the elements to make it happen. The board of governors carefully vetted the project and decided to proceed. But then they turned to management to make it happen.

For 40-plus years, I had been engaged in leading Christian ministries. I had learned how to work with others, but raising funds was most often done by a very few, and often left up to me. This time it was different. The magnitude of this project forced me not to be so self-reliant. It woke me up to the real need to trust and work with others.

It wasn't that teamwork was foreign to me—indeed that has been my style and pattern in ministry. And it has been a source of joy. But there was something different that time around. Maybe because I was older, or that I had come to see I didn't know enough to make it work.

I saw within our project team an enormous uplift in working together. Hope accrues. Wisdom accumulates. Faith projects into the future. Insights push away arrogant pride. Enthusiasm is catching. Reliance on the Lord assured us all. As a team, we shared disappointments and celebrated victories. I learned more about this side of leadership in that time than in my whole life. I thought I knew what it meant to work together. This team taught me every day, lessons I wished I'd learned earlier.

Prayer—

Dear Lord, Creator of community, world's First Manager and Coach, how fatigued we get when we forget we fly best when together. The hard lessons of "going south alone" are that we might not make it, and if we do, it takes all winter just to get up the strength to go back north in the spring. So Lord, teach me the wisdom and joy of flying—together. Amen.

Blinded by Goals

It was the 100-yard dash at the Olympics. The nine lined up and at the sound of the gun were off—except one boy who fell and lay on the racetrack, crying. The other eight heard him and stopped. One runner with Down's syndrome leaned over and kissed him. The others lifted him to his feet and together the nine, arm in arm, walked to the finish line. The entire stadium stood and applauded. This was no ordinary Olympiad—this was the Seattle Special Olympics.

Those who know me recognize my personality type. While there are at times unfair accusations levied against those of us dubbed "Type As," there's something to be said for its descriptive accuracy. It's for that reason this Olympic story grabs hold.

I make no apology for focusing on goals and working to achieve them. The old line "with no goals, that's what you'll achieve" is true. Such focus, however, can blind us to anything else. Other issues of tenderness and loving acceptance of people in need are too easily ignored.

A fellow airplane passenger told me of his son with Down's syndrome. I foolishly said, "That must be quite a burden for you." He looked at me with disbelief. "You don't understand. Those with this syndrome are, in my mind, the closest to what God created as our first parents. No one brings me joy as my son."

I was embarrassed and rightly put in place.

I've watched parents and grandparents of children disabled and seen the outpouring of love and affection. It's as if the greater the need, the greater the resource. Those who are needy have ways of releasing in our lives unmined gifts of eternal substance. Henri Nouwen told me that moving to Toronto to serve challenged adults at L'Arche Daybreak did more for his life and service than he was ever able to render.

In leading, we get mired in the job, the responsibility, the tasks that need to be accomplished. What evades our peripheral vision are relationships that need tending. If I miss that, I miss what in the end is our witness as Christ's community in the world.

Prayer—

Lord Jesus, today in the headlock of agendas, the rush of deadlines, the anxiety of not wanting to miss what people count on me to do, hold me in the simplicity of childlikeness, so the "what-is-now-here" and "what-is-yet-to-come" Kingdom is what grips my attention, ever leading me to Your intents and goals. Amen.

As a Child

Neoteny: The retention of youthful qualities by adults.

—*A zoological term*

"I'm drawn to this concept of neoteny: a quality of engagement in which the world is as attractive to me as a 68-year-old as it is to an active preschooler" (Bennis and Thomas in *Geeks and Geezers*).

Brycen, our young grandson, sees life through the eyes of Bob the Builder, a cartoon construction character who can build and fix anything. This loveable, energetic grandson is a hopeless romantic, convinced that there's nothing he can't do. Not burdened by failure, made cynical by the frivolous or become cautious by the unknown, he models this "quality of engagement."

Having seen it all, being exposed to the hyperbole of televangelists, listening to the partisan polemics of politicians and feeling the disabling hurt of personal failure, life too easily slips into the tactics of caution as much for a 34-year-old as a 60-year-old.

Leadership requires that we purposefully incline our hearts to the child, not the adult. Maturity notwithstanding, Jesus presses us to be as a child—to overcome the anxious "why?" with the hopeful "why not?" (Mark 10:13-16).

"In spite of illness, in spite even of the archenemy sorrow, one *can* remain alive long past the usual date of disintegration if one is unafraid of change, insatiable in intellectual curiosity, interested in big things, and happy in small ways" (Edith Wharton in *A Backward Glance).*

Prayer—

Dear God, Creator of the forever-young, continue Your work of recreating in me an untarnished spirit of trusting You beyond the myopia of age and experience, so that I may see and be part of the wider horizons of Your calling and blessing. Amen.

Discerning the Times

Mission, Strategy or Tactics?

"People discover and respond to the future as much as they plan it."

—*Ronald Heifetz*

Two former prime ministers of Canada—Jean Chrétien and Paul Martin—reflected on what success meant to them. Chrétien, the tough old codger, gave no room for any thought that he'd been pushed around. He seemed to love his use of power. He dealt with the hand played him. No big vision—just running a government as he saw fit.

Martin, outvoted after a short stint in running a minority government, was captured more by great ideas—those he believed should be of compelling interest for the federal government.

It doesn't take long to learn that as much as we might have a clear plan of the coming months and years, inevitably surprises, crises and opportunities cross our path, either pushing us in new directions, or so attracting our interests that they outshine what had been previously decided.

And therein lies the challenge: When is it right to abandon our well-considered plans and take a chance on new options?

Here's the question to ask: *Is this about mission, strategy or tactics?* If it's about the essence of one's call (mission), then it requires fundamental reconsideration of what we're about. If it's about strategy, then the question is *How will this relate to our plans?* If it's about tactics, then the question is simpler: *How will this affect what we're doing now?*

Chrétien was about tactics. Driven by holding on to power, he missed opportunities vital to the good of the country. Martin had so many missions that his strategy seemed vague, and in the end, the electorate didn't know what he wanted to do.

Mission needs sufficient breadth to handle the future. If too narrow, disasters or opportunities may derail. If your mission is to explore space, going to Mars is a strategy. If Mars becomes inaccessible, the mission isn't called into question—the strategy is. The mission is wide enough to handle inadvertent matters. We can decide to go elsewhere.

The future throws at us bizarre and wonderful realities beyond anticipation. Caught with a narrow or fuzzy mission, we might end up grabbing at what seems to work, and run right by what comes our way. The value of a strong mission differentiates that. So we need to ask: *Is it about mission, strategy or tactics?*

Prayer—

Father, Lord and Spirit, God in Three, all knowing of now and then, may the wisdom of Your eternal knowing be ours today as we sift through the surprises, disappointments and opportunities, so discernment will guide our response. In Your strong Name, Amen.

Beyond My Agenda

"Where is the line between loyalty and jealousy?"

—*Janet Clark*

Leaders, to a fault, are deeply loyal to their call and enterprise. What matters most to them is what they give their lives to. So it's not surprising when I hear of another ministry doing well—and worse, when better than us—the inclination is to be modest in praise, if at all. How small and stunted is the spirit that can only celebrate when it's us. Yet that too is the human condition.

Joshua complained to Moses that two men were prophesying—men who weren't part of the 70 chosen by Moses. He asked, "Moses, my lord, stop them!" Moses saw this for what it was: "Are you jealous for my sake?" (Numbers 11).

This happens in various ways. We talk with a colleague, and all they do is talk about their issues, successes or needs. And little or no time is given to ask us about our needs, feelings or priorities. They are consumed by their own agenda.

Or in reporting numbers, we inflate. Our loyalty produces action that says, "God is really only concerned about this ministry. We're the only ones that have the vision and capacity to do what God wants done." It is at its simplest, self-promotion. But at its heart is not so much loyalty, but an attitude driven by jealousy that finds its root in pride. If I could only see who I am from space. Perspective matters. As big and important as I consider my enterprise, in the wider scheme of things, it really is small.

Crowded by those I try to please, driven by my responsibility to make sure this enterprise works, overcome by the fear that others may pass me by, I am railroaded from what is good and important—loyalty—into jealousy. I may try and hide it. But others see it for what it is.

Loyalty is a quality I admire, and one I look for in others. What a jewel standing out among the flawed and discoloured stones of jealousy. To shift metaphors, it's more of an issue than just drawing a line in the sand between loyalty and jealousy. What I need is to dig a crevice of such frightening proportions between the two that I cross it only in desperate foolishness.

Today, celebrate with those He's blessing, even if what they're doing seems to crowd in on what you think is legitimately yours.

Prayer—

My big, expansive God, hold me in Your place of seeing, so with open eyes and heart I see life from the vantage point of Your self-interest. For as Your interest dictates my calling, I can then shuck off those nagging spirits of jealousy and truly rejoice in the successes of others—including those close to my calling—and with joy refuse the temptation of even thinking of crossing the line. Amen.

Is Complaining My Right?

"Complaint is the soil in which seeds of destructive attitudes are planted."
—*Stan Walters*

Eaton's department store built its grand enterprise on the basis that customers could return their merchandise for a full refund. Complaints for them became opportunities for winning customer loyalty. It was an idea unheard of at the time and became the winning formula for their enormous success. They turned an adversarial attitude into customer loyalty.

That's okay for a smart sales organization, but what does complaining do to our lives as leaders? Part of the leadership function is to serve as a repository for the complaints of our publics. We collect negative musings of our staff and community with a smile and nod of the head, all the while listening for a salient whisper of deep significance. No, we don't play games. But we do learn to keep our mouths shut and listen intently.

But how do I resolve my own complaints that are fair, and even those that aren't? We see those whose lives are encrusted by complaints that form over their personalities like a nasty and life-defeating film, keeping the oxygen of life itself from their needed renewal. "Oh, dear God, keep me from becoming that," I pray. But how?

I do it by realizing leaders have no right to complain to staff. That isn't in their job description. To let ourselves complain scratches at our credibility and trustworthiness. To be human and show self-revelation is good. To let our community know of our humanity, and how life digs raw at us too is good, in measure. That's different from complaining.

Our inner life as soil incubates complaints, which will in time produce weeds preventing nourishment for what matters. My life will soon become a sorry sight, out of touch with grace and beauty. Complaining acts like blight. Several years ago, blight affected the potato fields of Prince Edward Island, where potatoes are to Islanders what oil is to

Albertans. They had no choice but to destroy the entire year's crop and start over.

Leaders are human. We too feel sorry for ourselves. We can list the unfairness of life. But if that becomes the ruling emotion, then we need to get out of leadership. Because if we don't, we not only infect ourselves, but others too.

Prayer—

Father of Gentle Reasoning, help me give up my small ambitions, and allow Your gracious presence to lift me from nagging inner conversations over how unfair life may be. Today, I release them into Your hands so the soil of my inner life will be free from the plagues of self-pity. Then, my Lord, I will know Your endorsement. Amen.

Burning Out?

"It's better to burn out than to fade away."

—*Neil Young*

My young adult world was underwritten by this maxim: "Burn out for God." Then we got smarter. We came to understand each of us has particular gifts. Appreciating what those gifts were allowed us to better focus on doing what we did best. Great logic. It revolutionized my self-understanding and gave freedom to become in ministry what I was good at. It helped shape how Lily and I raised Murray and Muriel.

The huge benefit in self-understanding is quite obvious. If I'm more gifted to teach than preach, in the end, people will benefit more from my focus on teaching, and I'll experience greater satisfaction. It's a win/win. What God has gifted me with, He expects me to hone to maximize it in service. That's obedience. Further, it glorifies God from whom the gifts come.

Good, to a point.

This logic fits those of us in economic and social environments where we can pick and choose. It smacks of middle-class opportunity and Western affluence. This begs the question: If you're an elder brother in a tribe in Kenya, does the same principle rule? If you were pioneering on the Prairies in the early twentieth century, does the same logic prevail?

I think it does. While middle-class privileges allow me to pursue opportunities undergirded by my gifts, it doesn't mean that in places where the same is not so, that the principle of giftedness is negated.

However, we're distracted when personal gifting trumps other considerations. When someone is drowning, you don't ask if you have the gift of rescuing. You jump in. When a job needs doing, it's done because someone rolls up their sleeves and does it. Self-selection on tasks can be a camouflage for a low work ethic. Laziness.

It may be that in retrospect, burning out for God isn't that illogical.

Prayer—

Dear Maker of self and Giver of gifts, help me to find abandonment in Your calling. I'm not wanting foolishness that self-destructs Your creation. But fearing the listing to the side of self-interest and self-preservation, I pray that the sound of Your voice will call me away so my ambition is indeed caught up in what matters to You. Amen.

Goodness, How Bad Is It?

"Evil rolls across the ages, but so does good. Good has its own momentum. Corruption never wholly succeeds...Creation is stronger than sin and grace stronger still. Creation and grace are anvils that have worn out a lot of hammers."

—*Cornelius Plantinga Jr.*

I've had enough of wars and natural disasters, murders and chaos, illness and death, separation and divorce. Sometimes it's too much. Is there any good in life? The trick of evil is to make it appear as if it were normal. News media love fires, murders and traffic accidents. Like moths to the light bulb, they can't resist. I admit it: I'm a bit of news junky. But now and then I need a mental wash. A respite. A shutting down. A fresh look.

There's good in the land. The earth is the Lord's, and all that's in it. Squatter's rights are not synonymous with ownership.

Hermeneutics is the science of interpretation. How we see forms what we describe to others. It matters hugely how we see and teach the Scriptures. It also matters how we interpret the world to others. Is the glass half empty or half full? Where we begin forecasts where we'll end up.

There are moments when leaders appropriately scare the daylights out of their people. But what is our predisposition? What is our perspective, our cultural hermeneutic? Have you noticed that the pendulum of secularism has swung out to an extreme and now seems to be swinging back? In the fear mongering and doomsaying of the world, God is omnipresent. His accompanying goodness pops up everywhere.

Creation existed before sin. Plantinga is right: grace is the overwhelming favourite. His metaphor puts in mind round-headed hammers tired and banged out of shape, while the anvil continues to take a pounding.

In today's dryness, we would do well to sniff the air for signs of His latter rains. In the smallest of ways, in the most surprising of circumstances, we can see His goodness at work. Goodness will win. It'll become the default of human behaviour. Some day. His day.

Today we focus and listen intently for signs of His Kingdom doing good.

Prayer—

God of the Good, Lord of the Cross, Spirit over all the ages, free us from seeing what others push us to see, from negative dispositions controlling our hearts. You're good, and when You made this habitation and called it good, You expected that to be our paradigm, to become our hermeneutic. For when the glass is half empty, Your ever-ready jug of goodness prevails. Amen.

Through the Fire

"Character cannot be developed in ease and quiet. Through experiences of trial and suffering can the soul be strengthened, vision cleared, ambition inspired and success achieved."

—Helen Keller

A blacksmith in Meadow Lake, Saskatchewan, boasted he could shoe any horse. That boast was tested when he was challenged to shoe a wild bronco. Three days later, the horse quietly submitted. My friend, Wayne Boldt, asked how it happened. "Simple," was the blacksmith's reply. "I simply hobbled the horse for three days, and when I went to un-hobble him, he saw me as his friend."

Of the most important lessons in your life, what has been their context? Did they take place when everything was going well? When everyone liked you? When the organization was flush with money? My experience is the opposite. As C.S. Lewis suggests, pain is God's megaphone to get our attention.

We learn in the rough and complex moments of life. That seems to be God's prime teaching form. Not because He gets His jollies out of our discomfort, but because our blockheaded stubbornness is mollified when—knowing we don't know enough—we drop our defensive posture to learn.

Football was my game. Mike Marushak, coach of the Bedford Redmen, was demanding. Running fullback in the old split-T formation, it was only when I was humiliated in our opening game that I knew I didn't know. "Okay, Stiller, are you ready to learn?" I was, and that year we won the provincial championship.

Are you in hard times? Listen to Paul: "When I'm weak, then I'm strong," (2Corinthians 12:10). This isn't a slick commercial. It's how the Lord does His teaching.

Prayer—

Teacher, Wise One from all eternity, while I would hope my learning could all be done in a climate-controlled room, I know too well that in the good times, I forget that I have much to learn. So Spirit of the Holy One, temper in me resilience to see Your hand holding on when it feels the pressure is too great. Amen.

Canary in a Coal Mine

"Leaders must challenge the process because systems will unconsciously conspire to maintain the status quo and prevent change."

—*The Leadership Challenge*

The status quo is what I think others are trapped in. Seldom does it occur to me that I'm the one who's stuck. The reason? As leader, I assume I'm sufficiently proactive to be aware of when life is being held up by the comfort of being comfortable. It isn't that experiencing comfort violates Kingdom mission. But I've learned that comfort could be the canary in the coal mine, warning us of danger.

Forty years ago, the book *The Comfortable Pew* warned the Anglican Church of its coming demise if the comfort of its preferential position in Canadian culture continued to rule its plans and organization. How prophetic.

What is it about comfort that makes it so deadly? Human nature. Comfort builds complacency. The balance between being at ease and feeling unease is difficult for organizations to maintain. If the congregation, organization or business is not edging out onto a ledge of increasing discomfort, the feelings of comfort are so compelling that they build into systems, protocols, and defence procedures that protect rather than agitate for creativity.

I treasure Christian community for it brings me a wonderful sense of belonging and acceptance. Comfort is something else. It breeds a false sense of faith, couching me in its folds of assumed ministry. Comfort can lead us to pretend that, because we believe the right faith and mouth orthodox words, Christ's Kingdom is alive and active.

As leaders, we're tasked with the responsibility of ensuring systems are under constant challenge and scrutiny. People depend on us to build into the annual calendar incursions of discomfort so we don't confuse the joy and peace of our calling with the complacency of comfort.

Prayer—

Father, Creator who calls us to co-manage Your Creation, we long for comfort in being Your children, accepted by the Beloved. Help us not to confuse complacency with the comfort we experience in being Your people. We confess we need to be unsettled when prone to protection. Stir us up, Lord. Amen.

A Fatal Pretense

"And on the right, eternity."

Driving west on Highway 407, a toll road north of Toronto, I was startled by that sign. Wondering what it was trying to sell, I saw in smaller letters the name of a cemetery.

Goodness. Those guys sure had the gall to push my nose into what we all know is coming, yet are working hard to avoid—death. I grudgingly admired their boldness in pressing drivers-by to that one undeniable fact—we die.

A few years ago, I wrote a book on death called *What Happens When I Die?* I tried the idea on a few friends in their 90s. I got nowhere. I also nosed around my preacher-friends, asking how often in the past five years they had preached on death and its possible life-after options. There was hardly a one.

So the question for leaders is this: *How conscious am I of my mortality? To what degree are the visions I define, the plans I construct, the operations I initiate, and the day-to-day activities I manage overshadowed by eternity?*

Most of us live with a sense of forever. As much as we may define strategy within timelines, do I, in my heart-of-hearts, work out its value using a measuring stick that includes eternity? There's value for leaders in keeping eternity in our sightline.

"And on the right, eternity" says, "Remember, you take nothing with you." While I'm generally content with my financial lot, I do, now and then, wonder where I might be if I'd done something else other than public ministry.

"And on the right, eternity" consoles me when it seems like I'm spinning my wheels. While others may view my work to be of little worth, it looks different when seen through the lens of eternity.

"And on the right, eternity" acts as a rebuke when I think that what I do is all that matters.

"And on the right, eternity" assures me that each day is not just another day, but a day of time eternity won't forget.

Prayer—

Eternal Father, Creator of life and Saviour of death, may I see today's life and calling on the wider horizon of Your being and promise not as a threat, but as a reminder that You, who brought Creation into being, and us—Your image—into life, will see to it that what we do won't be discounted or forgotten. There's an eternity in which all You intended for us in Creation will be realized. And so today in leading, Spirit of God, may the thought of eternity be a reminder of Your promise—so that in remembering, I continue to trust in Your provisions for this day and give of my best. Amen.

How Am I Doing?

"I will consider, as if I were at the point of death, what procedure and norm I will at that time wish I had used in the manner of making the present election. Then, guiding myself by that norm, I should make my decision on the whole matter."

—*Ignatius Loyola,*
Founder of the Society of Jesus (Jesuits)
in Spiritual Exercises

I stood by the bedside of a friend in the late stages of cancer. She talked openly of her life and what it looked like from her vantage point that day. Regrets and wishes notwithstanding, she saw her journey as making sense from this now, most riveting moment.

Stephen Covey takes us to the end of the continuum, suggesting we evaluate today's actions by how they might appear to those who stand by our coffin at the end of life. Some days are filled with chattering issues, decisions, unexpected interlopers of people and ideas that throw us off track. With hardly a second to consider my response, I feel like a government minister in question period, blindsided by an unexpected question from the Opposition. If I saw some of my responses played on the evening news, what I said may look un-Christ-like. And said for all to hear!

What then helps me respond that corresponds to what is good? It's not the question. It's not the moment. And it's not environment. It's internal.

Chris Lowney in *Heroic Leadership* chronicles the life and ideas of the remarkable 450-year-old organization of Jesuits. Loyola, in crafting disciplines for its members, required the daily habit of reflecting on what you did that very day. This conditioning triggers a daily assessment. You aren't allowed to push the actual process of reflection out to that in-the-future moment that never really comes.

As much as I'd like to cast off those failures with "Well folks, that's just me," the discipline of daily reflection allows the Spirit to act within the sphere of my current memory, even as we discipline children within memory of their disobedience.

It triggers a spin on the environmental adage: hope eternally, love daily.

Prayer—

Dear Father, the One in whom resides all I need for goodness this day, may today's lessons not be lost in the forgetfulness of tomorrow's yesterday. May I instead be willing in reflection to remind (myself) and be reminded (by the Spirit) of Your will, so that in my tomorrow, there's a progression that surely and inevitably leads to the purpose marked and lived by Your Son, whom we call Lord. Amen.

Slow to Hire–
Quick to Fire

The Toughest Job As a Leader

"Slow to hire—quick to fire."

—*Archie McLean*

It seems so harsh and un-Christian. Brutal. A Darwinian character surviving as the most fit. One of the most rudimentary roles of leadership is to recruit, hire, assign and evaluate. Most of us have never taken a course in human resources, and we are less fit as a result. It should be a primary course for anyone with an inclination to lead.

We do it badly, I think.

Visionary leaders are inclined to move forward. Impatience, a common ailment too many have, shifts recruitment into high gear. Here's where one of my most grievous leadership flaws shows up. I'm in too much of a hurry. If someone comes along and shows interest, I'm interested too. If they believe they can do the job, I believe too. I want them to succeed. In untendered optimism, I sometimes jump too quickly and in the end, people get hurt. Slow to hire wasn't what I was known for.

And quick to fire? I was even worse at this because I felt sorry for the person. Also, in their failure, I failed, for I was the one who had signed their contract. And in their failing, the organization suffered and was set back. And the longer I waited to let them go, the worse it got.

I don't hear anyone quibbling about the first line. *Slow to hire* makes sense. But *quick to fire* seems like such rough justice.

As hard as it may sound, it's more Christian (given severance is fair and generous) to let someone not meeting the standard go early than to hold on. Most who aren't working out in their assignment know it, if they've been getting regular honest and reflective reviews. To leave them hanging in the frustration they cause others and themselves is unfair. I came to see that my reluctance to move a person not serving well ended up being unfair to them and the organization.

Given we provide caring and life-enhancing settlements to allow them to move forward into what works for them, being *quick to fire* isn't just good—it's best.

Prayer—

Dear Life-giver of talents and responsibilities, as leader and manager, may I see the importance of fairness and integrity in doing what a leader is called to do. Help me face the unpleasant task, knowing that it's mine to do. And in the doing, love and care for those who need to work elsewhere, knowing Your calling and leading is also in the tough job of having to lead. Amen.

Making a Successful Hire

"There's no such thing as 'Ten Easy Steps' in making the right hire."

—*From my journal*

Two accelerators drive recruitment: excitement in finding a new person who offers refreshing possibilities, and desperation in choosing the right person, knowing a wrong hire may upset the apple cart. So how do you go about making a successful hire?

Accept this reality—you won't bat a thousand. John Wallace, president of an international personnel search firm, reminded me that if as president I'm successful more than half the time, that's an average success rate. Finding the right hire is tough, so cut yourself some slack.

Decide if you need a pro who has done the work successfully elsewhere, or, if you're in a draft period, look for one whom you can help move up into the pro ranks.

Go beyond your immediate circle. New blood is a stimulus. Inbred hiring reduces the "genetic" pool of competence. Resist the urge to hire the latest one walking by your office.

Don't allow we-need-you-right-now anxiety to shortchange the time needed to search, select and confirm. Be slow at it. (This so cuts against my grain: *If it needs doing, let's get it done now* is my mantra. Wrong, as I've learned too often.)

Don't let first impressions be the judge. Malcolm Gladwell, in his best-seller *Blink*, says while our first impression is generally right, don't be fooled. Take into account all the means available in research, evaluation and testing.

Describe to the hire the accomplishments which that in your view will define success. Keep it clear, concise and concrete. No fuzzies here.

Give yourself breathing room in the contract. Discuss early what the break-off will look like if things don't work out.

The question then becomes *Yes, but where's the leading of the Lord in all this?* Everywhere. His leading is not divorced from testing, evaluation and research. Discernment is needed to sort out our unspoken preferences with competence, ability and leading. The Lord expects us to make the choice, all the while enabling us through His Spirit.

Prayer—

Spirit, Recruiter, Leader and Guide, in the hurry of figuring out who's best, hold me back from quick hires. In the maze of trying at the start to see if it'll work out, may the resources of others, insight, and tough analysis help form a decision that's best for the person, the position and the calling, all so that what You have in mind in doing through us here and now, is realized. Amen.

Making a Graceful Fire

An oxymoron? How can one be graceful in letting a person go?

By beginning well. If you finish badly, it may be because you started badly. The start forecasts the finish. The result is as good as the beginning. "Quick to fire" is not an organizational principle designed to get you as leader out of a jam. Rather it's a line that reminds us that the beginning is key.

Setting up the hire with a plan for success includes finding a way to end it, if the hire fails. There's always a chance it won't work. (There are exceptions and interventions beyond our control: organizational transitions and blow-ups or behaviour by the person we could not have forecast, to name only a couple.)

So set in place from the start how the end may look. In the employment contract, spell out how and what will happen if it doesn't work. Begin with clarity, understanding, and planning on how it might end. Keep in mind some core values:

- The hire is to be afforded dignity.
- The hire is to bring strength to the mission and outcomes of the organization.
- The organization is to be honourable in its assignment, regular reviews and honest feedback.
- The hire is to do what's expected, to work to become a "fit."

"Quick to fire" reminds the employer to act on what isn't working—either figure out what's wrong, make a reassignment, retrain, or provide an honourable means by which the person is let go. When it doesn't work out, with regular and honest reviews, neither the employer nor the employee will be surprised when an end is called. Most (at least in senior positions) whose leaving I've had to work out have known it was best for them to leave. They weren't surprised and were, for the most part, relieved.

Holding a person because you feel sorry for them or are unwilling to make the tough decision harms both the person and the organization. Leadership leaves you no choice but to decide when and how.

There are two factors that make such a tough job work. First, allow them (if the reason is not of a moral dimension) the opportunity to resign. Second, be generous in your settlement. The least expensive part of this is generosity.

Prayer—

Father of all work, You call, inspire, gift and affirm us in our work. Help me as leader to anticipate what might be an ending, and, in so doing, keep in mind the importance of allowing people (when possible) to understand the real reasons for leaving, so that in their future, they'll know better what to do and not to do. Amen.

Hope: A Bias to Succeed

"Energy as it is subjectively experienced is not derived from the chemical properties of food, but is the decision to have the courage to be, the commitment to exist. Energy is self-chosen, self-started, self-initiated. Its source is not visible to us, for we are it. Further, the energy we can summon—from sheer free will, self-discipline, determination, resoluteness, or guts—appears to be inexhaustible."

—Peter Koestenbaum

What saps your energy? What is it you do that when finished, you end up feeling you have nothing more to give? It's complicated. What I do know is that without certain elements in my life and schedule, anything I do drains me.

What are those elements? For me, they're freedom to initiate; freedom to create; freedom to get out in front. I can go through an unending list of meetings, attend personnel reviews, write fundraising letters and make countless donor calls, and not feel weary. But if within calling distance I don't have tasks that draw on my core sense of freedom to lead, then everything I do becomes dead weight. Burnout for me isn't overwork or administrative detail—it's when activities keep me from the creative edge of exercising freedom in leading.

Freedom produces vision, which in turn creates energy. Like riding a bicycle creates momentum to stay upright, so does leading with freedom create vision. Freedom and vision are not synonymous but inseparable realities. In exercising freedom in leading, your mind runs down the *what-ifs*. With the right and responsibility to lead, *Where are we going?* becomes the question.

Freedom exercised by leadership produces copious amounts of hope. Hope is the emotional environment in which belief and faith operate, and becomes the operational setting for members of the business or organization. Hope has a way of moving people from seeing the glass as half empty to half full. It sets a bias toward succeeding. It invites the activity of the Spirit into the enterprise. It begins with the assumption that we aren't alone. It sets in place an emotional continuum that builds momentum upon momentum.

This collects people together with a common will to act. Hope enables them to see the possible achievement of vision, and it becomes theirs. Within the personalizing of what *could* be, hope allows each person to translate that into what *will* be. Rising out of energy produced by the leader having freedom to lead, the stage is set for the community to operate with a divine optimism shaped by hope and not hype.

Prayer—

Dear Creator Lord of all that is, help me and us as a group to understand the importance of leadership needing freedom-in-responsibility to lead. May hope resting in You, the One-who-started-it-all, fire our hearts and imaginations with what might be. Amen.

No Perfect Workplace

"You can do everything with bayonets, Sire, except sit on them."
— *Talleyrand to Napoleon*

I'm a sucker for new gadget-tools, especially those amazing toolbox-in-a-single-gizmo ones. You know the kind: you flip out this arm, undo that collar, turn around the other appendage, and wonder-of-wonders, before you is a tool to fix anything.

Sometimes people who join religious organizations too often assume that they're entering a perfect place of Christian love and generosity where goodwill and happy times prevail. When they come up against grumpy supervisors, discover a pay scale lower than another, and all kinds of other human realities, they resort to a variety of accusations or criticisms.

What's unfortunate is that those who believe all will be well in a Christian organization are at times disappointed. They assume that Christian faith makes everything good and right. However, an organization is about getting something done. It's not an excuse to hire people so they can work within a Christian environment. That kind of environment is good, but it must have an end-of-the-day purpose.

It's not unfair or unreasonable to expect that organizations centred on the witness and life of Jesus Christ foster His kind of likeness. Nor should we downplay the importance of treating people as we expect Jesus would. And neither is it that being human lets us off the hook. We can't protest criticisms with an "All well and good, but being human means we aren't perfect either!"

The issue is this: Leadership requires us to help employees understand that being "Christian" isn't a magic tool, eliminating failure or annoyance.

Beware of those who in joining Christian organizations assume that all is well because of faith. Free them early of such notions. Take time to help them see that their own human condition needs the support of others who themselves need help from them. Everything has its purpose.

Prayer—

Father, in constructing organizations in the Name of Your Son, keep us all from searching for quick and simple formulas. Help us to see You at work within others and within this group of which we're a part. May we be Your instruments of grace and mercy to each other. Amen.

Knowing When to Go

"Sometimes to grow, someone has to go."

—*Archie Brown*

I asked my friend Archie what the turning point was in the great success story of Canadian Tire. Archie had worked in the head office in the early days before he became a dealer in Barrie, Ontario.

"It was when Alfred Billes took over from his brother John."

"Why?" I asked.

"Sometimes to grow, someone has to go," he replied.

The law of the jungle? Moses didn't move the Children of Israel into the Promised Land for good reason. He led them from captivity; Joshua settled them in their new land. It takes different skills for different needs. David built Jerusalem; Solomon, the temple. John built the foundation; Alfred knew how to make it grow.

So when is it time to go? And how do you know? When is it time to get out so someone else can take things to a new level? I've wondered. For several years I worked with a team in rebuilding and setting a new vision. Knowing when my time was over wasn't obvious to me.

Yes, leadership is critical to the well-being of an enterprise, but let's not forget that each leader has their own limitations. Each brings to an era what's unique to their capacity. But then comes the moment when it's time to move on, letting another with their gifts and skills lead for the next era.

Prayer—

Father who sees all, who I am and what I'm not, and who knows the needs for this enterprise today and tomorrow, keep me from believing that only I can do what's needed. This work is Yours. Your

Spirit superintends. Help me see what this ministry can be to Your Kingdom beyond my era. And may I know joy when another leads successfully. Amen.

When Should I Resign?

"I need discernment when looking for a new place of ministry or vocation. For in my search, the need may not be so much a call for a geographical cure as much as a call for a cure of a different sort."

—*From my journal*

When is it time for a leader to pick up from where you are and go to the next place? This question crosses the minds of pastors on many Monday mornings. How do you discern if you need to leave these people, this organization or business, this calling, this city, town or country? Why did I fail to know?

I was raised in a church community that expected ministers to move to different churches at least every five years. So I asked my father. He said, "You'll just know." After 16 years with Youth for Christ, I didn't. The leadership team knew before I did that it was time for me to leave.

Those in religious groups are blessed and cursed by prayers of "finding God's will." Blessed because it's powerful to know the Lord is leading—and cursed when it becomes an excuse to get out of an unhappy, failing or boring situation. Or a rationalization in the wintertime to go from the frigid Prairies to the balmy West Coast, or as a diversion on Monday mornings for a minister to wonder, "Is this the time to move on?"

My first lesson was don't ignore signs of boredom. As leaders, passion is high on our vocational graphs. If we aren't motivated, we become useless and potentially dangerous. The second was frustration and fatigue may not be signs that it is time to leave.

During moments of discomfort, an earlier, clear call was one hinge I couldn't unscrew. So I hung on. That was the cure I needed. Life is tough. Leadership is sometimes overwhelming. The very thought of sitting in another seat, collecting bi-weekly pay stubs, and letting someone else worry and anguish over impossible budgets and unhappy staff, was appealing.

Leaving earlier would've been wrong, even though at times thinking about it felt good. So how do I know the difference? I don't, any more than my father could tell me.

I can offer you this: His Spirit makes me—"Brian, the servant of Jesus Christ" (Romans 1:1)—know that my callings are within His mind and plans. His tutoring happens in the dilemma of wondering when to leave, where to go and what to do. Being His servant includes learning to follow when we don't know.

Prayer—

Dear Lord, Master and King, I feel juvenile over my fumbling attempts to find Your calling. I know self-interests can interpret my wants for Your calling. How less than ideal or good those interpretations can become. And yet You call. You lead. You equip. You empower. In my searching, give me boldness to press on, with humility to listen. Amen.

Beyond Faults

"Look out for the good things, not the faults. It takes a good deal bigger-sized brain to find out what is not wrong with people and things than to find out what is wrong."

—R.L. Sharpe

Many of us in teaching the children's lesson have used this object lesson. Taking a blank sheet of paper, we put a black dot in the middle. Then holding up the paper, we ask the children, "What do you see?" You'll be lucky if any will say, "A sheet of paper." The black dot gets their attention every time.

Newspapers see life through that kind of lens. So too do nightly and 24-hour TV and radio news reports. The worst is reported first. Fire, accidents and guns get top billing.

This is where your definition of leadership kicks in. Here's mine: *The stewarding of vision and resources in the doing of good.* The operative word is "stewarding." We're called to merge a compelling future reality—"vision"—with resources to achieve that vision.

The toughest job for a leader is to end someone's employment. We most often have to do it because the person doesn't have the skills we need. While everyone we work with has inadequacies, as steward it's our job to see if strengths outweigh inadequacies. We recruit and then hire based on hopes. Regardless of how careful our due diligence is, we don't always get it right. Eventually, we see flaws, inabilities and limited capacity. Then we have to decide if their strengths outweigh their weaknesses.

Responsible as we are for the well-being of the company or organization, we enter into their lives, attempting to reconfigure their tasks to affirm and encourage. Beginning with searching for their best side may save time, resources, their sense of dignity and the working environment.

Here's the challenge: To countermand the impulse to always critique, and to not allow weaknesses to overshadow strengths, so people know we cherish what's good in them.

Prayer—

Spirit of God, You who see the good, bad and ugly of me, teach me to see with Your eyes. At my best and worst, You make me Your temple. Lord, give me eyes to see what's good and valuable in others. May they in turn be lifted in faith, and fueled with passion for the work we do together. Amen.

Perspective Matters

The Other Side of the Brain

"Wonder is the only launching pad for exploring this fullness, this wholeness, of human life."

—*Eugene Peterson;* God With Us

Pragmatism is an accurate description of the ruling paradigm of many leaders. In politics, it's called *realpolitik*. In business, it's called the bottom line. Trained to read balance sheets rather than music scores, leaders are bred to "make the trains run on time." Caught in a small vision, we shrivel up. As our life shrinks, creativity is lost. What then do you do to keep from being led down such narrow paths? Nurture wonder.

We were a family of five children. Dad was a "bishop," overseeing small churches in Saskatchewan. Money was scarce. When we made eight years of age, each of us got jobs. And seemingly there was money enough for what mattered. It didn't occur to us at the time that a particular action on the part of our mother was rightfully placed in the "wonder" category.

A young classical pianist was coming to Saskatoon. His name was Glenn Gould, later to become the most famous of Canadian pianists. Mom told us we had tickets to his concert. Out of her grocery money, she had saved enough to make sure we kids heard this young prodigy. Our small Pentecostal church, resonant with gospel, and country and western music, was hardly the breeding ground for classical music. She knew her children needed something else.

Her push to entice us to appreciate more than the rock 'n roll of Elvis Presley and Buddy Holly, or the guitar-strumming ballads of Johnny Cash, helped build a love for music-wonder. Music of Bach, Rachmaninoff or Oscar Peterson—with a little Bill Gaither thrown in.

What is your best way to wonder? Life doesn't arbitrarily find us and push us into wonder. It may happen on a starry summer night. But such episodes are only occasionally caught. Wonder is a sought-after launching pad. It takes conscious effort to find time, to look for spaces in which we shift from a deadline pattern to musing and marvelling.

Build wonder into your life. A concert. Time in the country. Stroll through an art gallery. Your leadership will absorb new texture. Your mind will see higher than the closest horizon. Your newly nurtured soul will surprise and inspire those you lead.

Prayer—

Wonder Maker, Creative Mind and loving Lord, instead of me being saddled in bureaucratic numbness of getting-more-done, help me find a launching pad of Your creative wholeness. In this world of Your genius and making, I wish my life to have layers of wonder, a life choosing to see, feel and believe. Help me actively step outside the work-ring of my own making into the wider wonder of Your love. Amen.

Being Real

"For a leader, there is but a grey line that divides hope from hyperbole."
—From my journal

"When does desire to give people hope in a desperate circumstance subtly morph into hyperbole?" asked a colleague. We were talking of the time in the '90s when a few of us were attempting to rescue the school from near-bankruptcy. Many asked me then if there was any hope the college and seminary would live. What was I to say? (I had been appointed interim president, was new to this world of education and didn't know the essential factors of its survival.)

When asked of its future, my default position was, "I believe it will survive." So what was that? Hope or hyperbole? Hyperbole is an exaggeration meant for effect but not to be taken literally. Hope is a feeling that what is wanted will happen. In biblical context, hope is an attitude that creates an environment in which faith is expressed and practised.

Leaders are called on to generate hope. We have to. People look to leaders to set the margins in which their dreams are lived out. And therein lies the importance of good judgment. How far do we responsibly go in creating hope without crossing the line of hyperbole? Without the hope of possibility, people's will to do shuts down.

An important part of our task then is discernment.

I dislike attempts to merge "think and grow rich" with Christian ideas as if they're one and the same. While there are principles of attitude you can learn in the marketplace, biblical hope is realistic, linked by the action of faith in a loving and trustworthy Sovereign.

When everything seems impossible. As the sky is falling in. In those moments, we judiciously offer hope that may not be realistic to some, but from a wide-angle view describes God-factor possibilities, and in so doing enlarges space for people to walk in faith.

Prayer—

Dear Spirit of Hope, Transcendent God for whom there are no ends to the landscapes of hope, as we walk with those for whom hope is a mocker, give us discernment to know how far we can push their boundaries. So as their toe touches the water, hope replaces despair. For You want us to see that our boundaries aren't Yours. Spirit of Wisdom, as we speak words of hope, may they not border on hyperbole, but on what's possible within Your own good world. Amen.

Is There Such a Thing As a Blueprint?

"There is a great misconception: God has a blueprint for our lives."

—*From my journal*

A mission organization opened its evangelism booklet with this well-meaning line: "God loves you and has a wonderful plan for your life." Its intent was clear and powerful. God loves us dearly and our lives are of enormous importance to Him. The inadvertent message, however, is that our future has been planned in detail, and all we need to do is find the road map and follow it.

I affirm God's sovereignty, His all-knowingness. John Calvin and others help unravel the nature of predestination. Most important! But as much as He knows our future, He could—if He chose—keep us clear from shoals, sufficiently far from trouble. Often, He doesn't. He allows us to choose, to make our own way.

During the 1995 Quebec referendum on separation from Canada, someone said, "Don't worry, God is sovereign." "And what has that got to do with how Quebecers will vote?" I asked. "Just because God is sovereign, does it mean that He doesn't allow us to make choices—be they right or wrong?"

To make God into a blueprint designer, and us—those made in His image—into blueprint seekers, reduces His *imago Dei* to puppets on a string. Reducing His plan for our lives into a blueprint theology overlooks the relationship dynamic between Creator and created. Our walk is by faith, not by sight. King Saul was reproved for seeking out the Witch of Endor's help to learn of the future (1Samuel 28:3-8). Why? He wasn't to know.

Prayer—

God of the Future, all-knowing Spirit, Christ of the Emmaus Road, nothing of tomorrow catches You by surprise. The future I'm not told, for Your pleasure is our trust in Your leading. The line from start to finish is not straight. In all times and places, I trust You to be there. Lifting when I fall. Correcting when I fail. Nudging when I stray. Showing Yourself when I feel alone along the path I'm being taught. For Your tutelage, I'll be forever grateful. Amen.

Taking Credit

"Some people assume that learning about God's bigness necessitates negative obsession with their own smallness. You might hear them say things like, 'I am not valuable' or 'I have nothing to offer.' Such statements do not honor the nature and authority of God; they demean it."

—*Kurtz and Ketcham,* Ascent of a Leader

I've had my fill of people saying, "Oh, it was none of me, it was all God." I know what's usually behind such verbal contractions—an authentic desire not to claim personal glory. That's fine and good, and I admire such intent. But good intent doesn't, by and of itself, produce authenticity. Wanting God to receive praise doesn't mean unintended mistruths are legitimate conveyors.

A virtuoso dazzles me with Rachmaninoff's "Prelude in C Sharp Minor." I explode with enthusiasm, and then hear, "No, it wasn't me. It was God." How dithering! How intellectually sloppy! No, it *was* the pianist who had highly developed skills. The person trained for years, was well rehearsed. Yes, God gave the talent—all of it is God's. God is praised when we take His gifts and with deliberate devotion, do well.

I'm so amazed when someone from the IT department arrives on the scene and in minutes fixes what I think is absolutely unfixable. God didn't sort through the many options and correct them. The IT staff did. And because they're gifted, God is praised for their good work.

Leadership is a craft, honed over years of learning and doing. We take His gifting and work at it, so that in the end, as we do well, God is praised. The more we as leaders reinforce how important others' refined giftings are to His Kingdom, the more they'll see themselves as conduits of His grace.

One day a rabbi, seized by religious passion, striking himself on the chest, fell to his knees before the ark: "I'm nobody! I'm nobody!" The cantor of the synagogue, impressed by this display, joined the rabbi on his knees with "I'm nobody! I'm nobody!" The custodian watching from the corner couldn't restrain himself. He joined the other two on their knees, calling out, "I'm nobody! I'm nobody!" The rabbi tugged at the sleeve of the cantor. "Look who thinks he's a nobody."

Prayer—

God of limitless creativity, unbounded by the small borders of our ideas, Maker of Your people, we're made to enjoy You forever so that in our joy, You're praised. Help us see concerts of life, crescendos of praise, crafted and executed by those You yourself made. You delight in us doing well, that which You created us to do. For when Your children are praised, we know You, our Father, are too. That for You, we believe, is Your pleasure. And it's Your pleasure we seek. Amen.

Seeing Reminders

"The only serious mistake we can make when illness comes, when anxiety threatens, when conflict disturbs our relationship with others, is to conclude that God has gotten bored in looking after us and has shifted his attention to a more exciting Christian, or that God has become disgusted with our meandering obedience and decided to let us fend for ourselves for a while, or that God has gotten too busy fulfilling prophecy in the Middle East to take time now to sort out the complicated mess we have gotten ourselves into. That is the only serious mistake we can make."

—*Eugene Peterson from* A Long Obedience in the Same Direction

In my early years of public ministry, I had a secret dream to accomplish something that I soon learned was outside the possible. A close friend shared the same dream, and he fulfilled it. Shadowed by his public success, I for a while equated my inconspicuous calling with being less important.

James and John, insecure that when the Kingdom arrived they'd be positioned below their expectations, asked Jesus for prime seating: one at His left hand and one at His right—executive VP positions (see Mark 10). Seems so foolish these centuries later. Was it that they wanted to be senior execs, or to be noticed by Jesus?

I need to be noticed. Not for significance—although that too is important—but for one important reason: If I don't feel God in my life and circumstance, ministry slips away.

As a leader, affirmation of His calling and presence matters. We have so many reasons to know of our Lord's careful watch in our lives, but like any other relationship, unless we feel a regular touch of love, we wonder, "Do I still have His attention?"

Figuring out the intricacies of Bible prophecy seems so much more intriguing than understanding the habits of a wayward heart. What matters more to God? Even in my failings, sins and obsessions, my life has supreme significance. The one of 100 sheep matters so much that the 99 are left until the one is found (Matthew 18:10-14).

Prayer—

God of Creation, You who spun planets into orbit, help me see reminders that You care about my life and work. May I more carefully do all for Your glory and approval—and not for notice or praise by friends and colleagues. I'm thankful that You love and see not just me, but all of us whom You lovingly link together as Your Kingdom witness. Amen.

Just Showing Up

"If I have done anything in my life, I have done it as a relative of the donkey that went its way carrying an important burden. The disciples had said to its owner, 'The Lord has need of it.' And so it seems to have pleased God to have used me at this time, just as I was, in spite of all the things, the disagreeable things that quite rightly are and will be said about me. Thus I was used. That is how I happened to be present and that was my work. I just happened to be on the spot."

—*Karl Barth*

Jay Kessler commented, "Sometimes leading is just showing up." Such a definition of leadership can be misleading. But it helps me understand—on days when I wonder what value I am—that people need me to be there.

There are days lacking the energy to drive a vision and full of apparently unnecessary appointments. I wonder, "Do they need me? In fact, do I really matter?" Then I show up and something happens, and surprise—*me being there mattered!*

Embedded in showing up is a conviction that we partner with the Spirit of God. Gifts, skills, strategies—and other tools of leadership—are effective in that they tie in with the intent, provision and activity of the Spirit. When Peter showed up at the house of the Roman military leader Cornelius (Acts 10), he had no notion of what the Spirit was doing. When he arrived, he found out. History rolls out the grand saga of God pulling the early Jewish Christian leaders over the racial fence into the world of Gentiles and Europeans.

We needn't flex our leadership muscles to remind us of the importance of leading. Sometimes God wants us to be in a place of His choosing to do what He knows needs done. Showing up isn't as irrelevant to leadership as we might sometimes think.

Prayer—

Father, on this day when what I do seems unimportant, may Your call to faithfulness overrule so that in walking in my world today, I might be where You want me to be, to do what You know needs done. Amen.

Get It Done

"There are times it takes the leader to make it happen."

—*From my journal*

In November 2004, my friend and well-known preacher Dr. Tony Campolo received a call from former president Bill Clinton, asking Tony to pray at the opening of his Presidential Library in Little Rock, Arkansas, the coming week. "Mr. President," Tony responded, "I'm sorry, but I can't. I'm speaking at a series of banquets for Tyndale in Canada."

That seemed to be the end of the matter.

Twenty minutes later, Tony received a call from the White House. "Dr. Campolo. This is George Bush. I need you to pray at the opening of the William Jefferson Clinton Presidential Library in Little Rock, Arkansas, next week."

Tony outlined the timing problem he had discussed with Bill Clinton just minutes before. This time, however, Tony knew he couldn't refuse a request from his president.

"Tony, give me the closest airport to your dinner on the Wednesday evening."

That night, after our Tyndale dinner in Kitchener, we drove south to Hamilton. As we pulled into the Hamilton Airport at 10 p.m., there on the tarmac was a jet waiting to take Tony to Little Rock.

There are times it takes the leader to make it happen.

Prayer—

Father, I recognize my calling and responsibility. Grant me Your wisdom to know what needs doing now, what can wait for another day, and what I alone can trigger into action. Help me not to procrastinate, but with grace and clarity of vision do what my calling and position require of me this day, in Your love. Amen.

Taking Risks

The Intersection of Faith

"A very religious Jew named Goldberg wanted to win a lottery. Every Sabbath he would go to the synagogue with this prayer:
God, I have been so pious all my life. Would it be so bad if I [won] the lottery?
The lottery came and went. Week after week, month after month, Goldberg would return from the lottery, empty-handed.
Finally, it was more than he could take.
God, I have been good all my life. What will it take for me to win the lottery?
The heavens opened:
Goldberg, give me a chance. Buy a ticket."

—*Thomas Friedman*

How are we to interact with God so our actions run alongside His will?

Leaders pray for His intervention in all sorts of things. And in so doing we evaluate what we ask for, wondering if it's a fair or reasonable request. Is it in line with what I know God would want? Am I only doing this for my personal benefit?

In the many courses offered by fundraising associations, I seldom heard talk about the role of faith in planning and execution. Steeped in a culture rooted in the need to master organizational skills, driven by the importance of strategic planning, or shaped by the need that as leader I get the "right people on the bus," planning with faith as a vital ingredient isn't usually included.

Of course we have stories of those who, in irresponsible acts of so-called faith, got themselves and others into difficulty, embarrassing the Gospel and hurting people. We can also recount people and times in which claims to "walk by faith" were made by some who did nothing—as if faith were made possible only when they sat with hands out, waiting for a miraculous provision.

Faith is not what we believe—it's what we do. It's within action that faith is experienced. It's not what we hope to realize—it's putting ourselves in such a place that only when He comes through, we make it. There's a distinct relationship between actions—which is the essence of faith—and knowing that without His enablement, we will fail.

Prayer—

Dear God, in whom we find our daily nourishment, and the One in whom my eternity is secured, may I learn the lesson of faith that presses me beyond a casual attitude or knee-jerk response of assuming my part in this journey is only to believe. You call us to partner with You, and in so doing, You expect us to lead with ideas and plans that necessitate, by faith, Your help. Amen.

Which Way in a Crisis?

"A leader, in dealing with an issue, has three possible options:

- *circumvention*—with the risk of backing into a potential crisis
- *frontal challenge*—getting out in front and becoming the "bearer of bad tidings" by introducing the crisis
- *riding the wave*—staying just in front of the crisis, anticipating the wave and trying to direct its power as it breaks."

—*Ronald A. Heifetz*

Most of us aren't usually forced to handle a crisis in public as does a prime minister or president. Away from the public stare, we at least have a measure of privacy in which we can shepherd the matter, albeit sometimes under the glare of staff, faculty, business acquaintances or donors.

However, be it in public view or couched within a smaller auditorium, how we deal with crisis is often a reaction determined by our personality, style or emotion. Count to ten and ask: *Which of the three approaches will I take?* None is sacred. No single one is best for all times. Riding the wave may at first seem to be somewhat like circumvention—a wimpy refusal to try the frontal approach.

When trying to rescue Tydale from receivership, we merged the frontal challenge and riding the wave into a co-ordinated duo. First, we told the bad news. And we decided to tell most everything often. Full disclosure of the problem would help us rebuild trust with many communities better than circumvention.

This we tied to riding the wave. Once the worst of the news was public, anything further we had to say could be coupled with what we were doing to handle it. The decade-earlier Tylenol crisis became our guide. Recall they had a problem with someone inserting poison into capsules. The company immediately pulled its product off the shelf and re-engineered the capsule into a solid, and as they did, they told the public. Soon, they recaptured their market share.

Religious, not-for-profit communities, are gun-shy to identify problems. We do our best to circumvent, moving people around, re-labelling the problem to mitigate the possible downside.

This market line has residual wisdom: "The first loss is the least loss."

Prayer—

Spirit of Eternity, Knower of the past and future, in my moment of crisis give me distance to see the facts, reflection to discern what approach best to take, wisdom to do it with measured speed and courage to carry it out, in Your holy Name. Amen.

When Afraid...

"If people knew at times how scared I am, would they trust me?"

—*From my journal*

What's the role of candour in the life of a leader? What's the balance between fessing up to those we are accountable to, and pressing on in faith and courage?

I've been in leadership since graduating from university in 1966. During my early days in Montreal as director of Youth for Christ, I had no substantial idea what to do. I was out of my depth. The youth ministry was bankrupt. Expo '67 was almost over. Moving vans were lined up ready to move English-speaking Quebecers down Highway 401 to Toronto. And with them a whole bunch of Christians from whom came our financial support. Quebec was about to feel the wrath of political fanatics.

I rarely mentioned my fears, but there were occasions when I needed the board of Montreal YFC to surround me with encouragement and love. I attribute learning how to lead as much from that group as any other. A critical factor was their willingness to let me make mistakes. And within those mistakes, to hold me in accountability and love.

Fast-forward 44 years.

So when *is* it appropriate to indicate how I feel? I don't know when, but I know it's seldom. It's an expression we use on rare occasions. Gratefully, I have six guys—we retreat twice a year—with whom I can freely and openly express my feelings. In confidence. To loving hands. With security. And for good purpose.

So why not tell my board or senior staff? Because that's not helpful in management. Central to leading is the activity of faith. It defines us like little else. It's what we bring to the enterprise. It's what our boards look to us for. They don't need to hear of my fears. They need the lift of my walk and trust in the provision of the Lord.

Fear is not the antithesis of faith. Confidence is. Fear is a fertile ground in which the seed of faith grows and overcomes. There's nothing wrong with being afraid. We're all fearful at times. Find the right person and time to express it, so that in facing it, you build skills to overcome it by faith.

Prayer—

Gracious Giver of Faith, by Your indwelling Holy Spirit may I stand in the face of frights and fears, knowing Your gift of faith is a never-ending source. Lord, give me boldness so I may see beyond the immediate skirmishes, out to the periphery where the great warriors of Your unending Kingdom are ever ready to assist. For in You, I am strong. Amen.

Self-fulfillment–a Misnomer?

"A modern assumption is that to have a calling is to experience self-fulfillment in that calling."

—*Douglas Shurrman*

I'm OK, You're OK of the 1970s soared on a societal craze for feeling good. Self-fulfillment became a litmus test for success. Christians are shaped by this cultural climate, interpreting God's call on the basis that it must lead to self-fulfillment. Nothing so belies the biblical call and turns spiritual well-being inside out than to assume that if we feel fulfilled, we must be within the borders of God's will. Or conversely, if we don't, we've missed it by a half mile.

It isn't that having a sense of fulfillment is not of our Father's interest. I'm not suggesting that having a deep assurance of what you do isn't good, nor am I saying that it's inappropriate to want to feel fulfilled. The context here is leadership—what you and I are called to exert from our gifting.

I've been asked—especially when I moved into academic leadership—"Brian, are you enjoying your work?" My only honest response was, "The question I wish you'd ask is 'Are you doing what you should be doing?'"

There are moments we feel rewarded, the blush of success, or our work is in concert with God's grand scheme. But that's not our best gauge. Good times are momentary. Some encounters leave me with self-doubt. Many decisions come by agonizing reflection. There are decisions that committees leave alone, that manuals don't solve. Leaders are called on to find closure.

Self-fulfillment may be a by-product of leading. But make it the test of being in God's will, and you're soon tempted to "hear" God's call to "sunnier" climates, to places behind the front lines, to people who appreciate who you are and what you have to offer.

I can't finish the eleventh chapter of Hebrews and then live with a sense of entitlement, that as God's servant, self-fulfillment is my right. "These were all commended for their faith, yet none of them received what had been promised" (Hebrews 11:39).

Prayer—

Dear Father and Lord, life seems crazy. My world chatters up a storm on being fulfilled. It's as if I need to buy its mantra if I'm to avoid being a misfit. I feel pulled. I so want to hear Your voice of approval—the only seemingly worthwhile reward. Yet in too many days, life struggles are out of sync with the assumption that leadership brings personal fulfillment. It's not often I feel this way, but in this prayer let me offer these words, by faith: "Dear Father, I'd trade feelings of self-fulfillment any day for knowing that in some modest way, my life is geared to fulfill Your calling." Amen.

New Steps

"Taking a new step, uttering a new word, are what people fear most."

—*Fyodor Dostoevsky*

It took our blue-eyed grandson Jacob some months before he was ready to leave the security of his mother's arms. Different arms, unfamiliar faces and strange smells got his chin quivering. He wasn't quite ready. It's not unlike my first day in elementary school, September 1948, in Tisdale, Saskatchewan. Walking up the stairs into the classroom was more than my fearful heart could manage.

Years later, standing on a platform, knowing that in a moment eyes will turn and ears will listen, I wonder, "Am I able?" That question now and then rears its haunting horns. Fleeting, but perceptible.

Comfort is contagious. Staying here, not venturing out, calms anxiety. But beware. Such comfort is not chicken soup to the soul—it's hemlock to the spirit. When a friend or colleague says, "I really don't like what I'm doing, but in ten years I'll have security," stop them. Warn them of their self-defeating logic.

Indecision—sometimes better called *fear*—becomes the rationalization of staying trapped. Be warned: Indecision doesn't become increasingly contagious because of age. I've seen it in the young too.

Among the many things we do as leaders, we work to prevent our organization or business from being comfortable in letting the tomorrows be as today. New opportunities open when we leave where we are for a place in which we have nothing to count on. In those moments and places there rises in us resourcefulness that'll surprise you. And the Lord, who by His Spirit has already visited places you've yet to go, will surprise you with His preparation.

Take that new step. Don't allow fear to be your day planner.

Prayer—

Loving Father, Rising Son of all Tomorrows, even though I'm confronted by fear of the unknown, help me push back the curtain and leave the Ur (Abraham's home) of my comforts, seeking out Your promise. Amen.

Living Out Possibilities

"It is a dangerous business to arrive in eternity with possibilities which one himself has prevented from becoming actualities. Possibility is a hint from God. A person must follow it...if God does not want it, then let him hinder it; the person must not hinder it himself."

—Søren Kierkegaard (1813-1855)
Danish theologian

I have mixed feelings about a theology framed by "possibility thinking." On the front side, I believe a mind open to possibilities sees what others don't. As an optimist, I relish in what can be done more than in the reasons why something can't.

My reluctance with the theology of possibility thinking is that it translates sin as negative thinking, and redefines our fallen nature into psychological disability. That's a huge mistake. By so doing, we end up commercializing the Gospel and shaping it into psychological hype. There may be underlying evidence that such a mindset works, but does that make it the same as being filled with the faith of the Spirit?

With that disclaimer, I'm drawn by Kierkegaard's insight. I have one life to live, and I want that life to count. At the sunset of my life, when I watch the wheelchairs rolling by me in the nursing home, what will I look back on? Flip that out into eternity. Will I see that the possibilities God put in my way had become realities?

Don't measure yourself against those whom our culture and history books call "great." Rather ask: *What am I allowing to hinder me from doing what's good and right? What are the possibilities at hand? A child to lead? A letter to write? A word to speak? A mission to support? A student in need of encouragement? A senior in need of a visit? A sacrifice to make so an idea might be born?*

We may interpret fear as God not wanting us to move forward. Kierkegaard reminds us to let God stop us from moving forward if He so chooses, but let's not stymie the possibility of moving something into actuality because of inertia or lack of faith. Instead, let's agree to arrive in eternity having lived out possibilities.

Prayer—

Triune God, Creator of all that is, Saviour and Renewer of life, help me shed the garments of fear and take on those of faith, so that I and those impacted by my vocation, mission and calling will be accelerated in the knowledge of You, compelled by the possibilities of Your own self. Amen.

Smoothing the Rough Edges

Reporting ROI

"What is true for leaders is, for better or worse: we are our own raw material."
—*Warren Bennis*

Nature or nurture: Where do I locate my abilities, interests and talents?

This I've learned is not an "academic" (i.e., irrelevant) debate. Jesus' parable of the talents (Matthew 25:14-30) is too graphic to ignore. In the parable, He tells of a master who gives three of his servants various amounts of money—talents: five, three and one—for investment, with the expectation of a profit upon his return. The amounts are significant. One talent equalled 20 years of labour. In today's currency, the five-talent servant's investment is equivalent to $4 million. Serious money!

The one who buries his single talent gets a tongue lashing from the master: "Throw that worthless servant outside, into the darkness, where there will be weeping and gnashing of teeth." Hold on, Jesus, for goodness sake. He didn't kill anyone! Serious business!

That's why my question isn't academic. Jesus took time to lay out His seriousness about gifts given, and if He does, we need to as well.

We begin with the inherent talent derived from genetic material as in-His-image (nature), and build with what infiltrates us from family, life experience and the Spirit's anointing (nurture). How can the two be separated? Scientists of all sorts of disciplines can't figure it out, so I won't try.

But I've learned that knowing your "raw material" can be helpful. While there's danger in being over-preoccupied with gifting, knowing what's mine can be an awfully good place to start. Are you intimidated by those with the "five-ers?" Their talents are so obvious. It's convenient to sequester and let jealously, fear, intimidation—whatever—rankle our inner composure so that we bury ours, at least for that time and place.

Jesus is tough. He borders on the edge. Avoiding a tendency to soften this seemingly harsh reality, we remind ourselves that grace is why we're accepted by the Beloved. But don't let this blunt call to accept responsibility for managing these gifts be lost in the warm fuzzies of religious chatter. He'll want to see our return on investment.

Prayer—

Master Investor, this picture seems too intemperate for how I prefer to see You, yet Your parable shows no half measure of requirements. As I examine the agenda of the day, may it not be a day like any other. With these gifts given from Your hand—enabled by discipline of mind and empowered by Your ever-indwelling Spirit—help me, Lord, to invest wisely. Amen.

Counterculture Faith

"A restless countercultural instinct to keep challenging the status quo was built into Jesuit heroism."

—*Chris Lowney in* Heroic Leadership

The American and Canadian Idol series capture the attention even of those I consider to be serious-minded Christians. I'm befuddled by this. But better I don't judge for I watch sports.

Culture is our womb, our social, linguistic sea in which we find life and meaning. It's a gift. But that doesn't mean it's always good or right. Culture, like humanity, is fallen. The cumulative effect of people living together ends up creating all sorts of good and evil.

One matter should concern us—the danger of falling into the assumption that the Christianity of North American society is closest to what Jesus has in mind. This blending makes us vulnerable in sanctifying our own sins. (The British did it in the nineteenth century and Americans/Canadians in the twentieth century.)

We too easily get absorbed by attitudes fuelled by a materialism and hedonism that give shape and meaning to this culture. There's so much good that arises within our North American world. We can point to all sorts of policies and opportunities that are outgrowths of this Gospel-influenced society. And that's good. But surging underneath our social experience are preferences that attempt to lead us far from Christ's Kingdom. Instinct is a spirit-enabled ability to know what goes against Kingdom values. And of all the skills that leaders need, it's instinct.

In the current debate over church worship patterns, both sides—traditional and emerging—are in danger of bowing to the culture. Traditional worship holds to what grew out of classical and popular culture of past generations, and emerging worship uses popular contemporary cultural forms. Both are in serious danger of lacking critical examination by being caught in their respective cultural views.

A Christian mind is by nature inclined to critique cultural norms.

Countercultural thinking can give room for the Spirit to help us see what most miss, fashioning an environment of creative ingenuity.

Leadership requires discipline to avoid assuming that the most obvious is correct.

Prayer—

Great Spirit of Jesus, hold us in Your word and Word, within the mind of the Father, and keep us from the trap of believing that either popularity or conventionality best shapes our witness of You. Amen.

Ready. Fire. Aim.

"No plan of war survives the first exchange of gunfire."

—*Carl Von Clausewitz,* On War

I admit to vacillating between two opinions. For my direct reports, I advise, "If your strategy hasn't been written out, it hasn't been thought through." Yet at times with an end goal sufficiently clarified, I'd find a way to do it, with or without a plan. Being high on the intuitive side, I love the zigzag of operation: "When one thing doesn't work, try another." Organizations need polarities of leaders. Visionaries who couldn't name a strategy if it hit them in the face, and managers who have no idea what it's like to see things from 33,000 feet. We need each other.

We need those who, in the rough and tumble of engagement, are driven by the goal so much that bungled plans don't throw them off. They know intuitively that life is never as it seems. Vision provides gravity that holds when all seems lost.

And while I may grind my teeth when asked, "Where's the business plan?" I know that without going through the steps a plan requires, if enthusiasm isn't balanced by careful thought, too often it'll end in disaster. The point is not to bypass planning. Rather craft a plan that anticipates what won't survive the first exchange of fire.

Religious organizations funded by donations are particularly vulnerable to a leader who's prone to lead only with passion. In such cases, leadership may, at first, get away with a lack of planning by simply cranking up salesmanship. Knowing people respond in giving more to passion than strategy, visionaries may avoid the rigorous and often boring task of labouring through the process of developing a plan.

Somewhere along the way of leading, we learn to find the polarities of vision and management, and build them into a union of mutual respect and activity. Given that the first shot inevitably changes what we hoped would be, we must not give space for the argument that success comes without planning.

I give thanks to God for those He brings into my life whose polarity gives balance to my tendency to "Ready. Fire. Aim."

Prayer—

Father, the One who knows today from the past, give me vision to see beyond my anticipations of today and tomorrow into the wider activities of darkness and light. In my striving, I know I can't anticipate all that is or predict what may be. But in trusting, I believe faith will rise above the changes, surprises and disappointments. Amen.

The Battle of Character

"It is sometimes frightening to observe the success which comes even to the outlaw with a polished technique...but I believe we must reckon with character in the end, for it is as potent a force in world conflict as it is in our own domestic affairs. It strikes the last blow in any battle."

—*Philip D. Reed*

Success and character are different realities: success, the achieving of what was intended; character, one's moral and ethical construct. How do we link the two?

Here's the problem. Some with character intact, when evaluated as leader, have achieved little. They're good and faithful, but show little accomplishment. Could it be their character is unblemished because they haven't been tested in places of stress and heat?

I bristle as popular writers, secluded in quiet reflection, craft their judgments on leadership away from the litmus test of doing. Neatly they prescribe symmetrical contours of leadership, sprinkled with "musts."

Don't misunderstand. I love moments when ambition and institutional self-interest submit to higher values. I treasure that rush when doing good. When others see ethical choices rule, a sense of well-being overtakes. But there are many times when success rules, fuelled by driving ambition. Like Moses. Like King David. Like Peter.

Ah, there's the rub. Character is not latent in personality or upbringing, precluding me from being an "outlaw." Rather it's a protagonist, battling my predilections to use "polished technique." Character is more than accrued personality. It's what I become when, seeking to achieve, I am countermanded by the good.

Do you notice how Billy Graham seems to act with humility? The issue isn't is he humble, but does he practise humility? When pride struts, humility as choice does battle. Little wonder we're called to "humble yourself."

Prayer—

Lord, Your very transcript describes King David "after Your own heart." His entrenched character flaws—which didn't keep him from You, or more importantly, You from him—weren't enough to block his desire or attempts to serve You. So today, Father and Lord, keep testing us in fire so that the stuff of character eventually prevails. Amen.

Ministry May Be a Poor Solution

William Towan, in writing on the role of religious leaders, especially those working in a church or parish said, "Salvation affects the whole of the psyche; to try to escape boredom, sexual frustration, restlessness, unsatisfied desire by searching for fresh tasks and fresh ideas is to attempt to seal off these areas from grace. Without the humiliating and wholly 'unspiritual' experience of parish life—the limited routine of trivial tasks, the sheer tedium and loneliness—there would be no way of confronting much of human nature."

I asked a psychology professor why there are such large classes in psychology. "One major reason," she said, "is that students from dislocated and fractured homes want to understand themselves."

Ah, could it be somewhat like why many of us end up in church and mission-agency ministry? It isn't a surprise that many of us working in the world of religious ministry are here because we're in search of answers to our spiritual questions, and quite frankly enjoy the spiritual nurture that accompanies such employment.

But here's the danger—when it becomes the means of solving what Towan warns us about. In ministry, we may delude ourselves with the illusion that in doing ministry, we're likely to solve our flaws and reverse our inclinations.

At one point in my ministry life, I went through a valley of unhappiness in my calling. I clearly knew I was where I was meant to be. So what was I to do? To leave would've meant running to Tarshish (Jonah 1). To stay loaded on increased disquiet.

I found a simple principle. The discipline of obedience mattered more to my maturing than did enjoyment. And further, this discipline in time produced joy.

The addiction of working harder can numb us to issues that need attention. Christ's transformative work reaches into every crevice in our lives. In trying to escape from "boredom, sexual frustration, restlessness, unsatisfied desire" with additional committees, deadlines, sermons and budgets, we deny place and presence of God to fulfill His promise. When we do, we lose.

Prayer—

Landowner, Manager, The One Who Calls, You didn't call us into Your vineyard to solve our inner struggles. We as leaders are here because You want something done—a mission fulfilled, a congregation loved, a school built. Even so, in the middle of leading, we need Your salvation. The unresolved errors, the tendency to be complicit with self-interests and gaps in character, need Your saving grace. I trust You for that today. Amen.

Leading Unafraid

"Jesuit heroism is not just a response to a crisis but a consciously chosen approach to life; it is judged not by the scale of the opportunity but by the quality of the response to the opportunity at hand."

—*Chris Lowney in* Heroic Leadership

Who among us knows from the start whether or not our chosen calling will lead to greatness, be it personal or societal? Most of us start out small, doing the menial, looking after the mundane. As much as our deepest desires are loaded with hope to do something great in life, we can't know if what we begin will lead to public significance.

Paul Henderson, the best known of Canadian hockey heroes, scored the winning goal in each of the last three games of the 1972 Canadian/Russian hockey series. The Russians had won the first games (played in Canada!), and it looked as if the Canadians would end up the losers. Unthinkable for Canadians who believe they own the game.

Henderson, a relative hockey unknown at the time, was chosen for the series. In the seventh and final game played in Russia, the game was tied with only 34 seconds remaining. Henderson's goal was voted by Canadians as the greatest moment in sports of the twentieth century. Paul told me he had hoped to be a good hockey player, but never expected it to come the way it did.

Most of us live in relative obscurity, grinding out the daily chores of our calling. What we don't know is the potential impact our life and work will have on people and society.

Life lived in Spirit-shaping choices does two things: it lifts the burden of trying to anticipate what has greater potential, and helps us settle into the Jesus-spirit of service. Wanting to be great or achieve greatness is refined, not squashed.

The Jesuit story, including its dark side, is a 450-year listing of people who were unafraid to accept the most daunting of calls. And in so doing, they brought change and influence to the world.

Prayer—

Dear Lord of Opportunities, as much as I wish to lead a life of significance, help me in this day, in the tediousness of my calling, to know that it's You who evaluates what's worthwhile and significant. In the meantime, give me Your wisdom to discern what's important, and courage for what's needful. Amen.

Leadership Is More Than Science

"The only thing that matters in art can't be explained."

— *Georges Braque, French painter*

We had a marvellous art curator at Tyndale. A fine painter, Sabrina Lowe helped expand my love of art beyond the impressionists Monet and Renoir to abstract art. Sometimes I look at abstract art and wonder, "Did the artist just throw cans of paint at the canvas?" They may have. But over time, I've learned to appreciate and even love some of it.

One evening, while sitting with a group of aspiring artists in downtown Toronto, I looked over at their sketches and wondered what point they were trying to make. Then I looked at my charcoal sketches and asked myself the same question. In conversation, I tried to explain. But words weren't enough.

Could the same be true in our leading? I was once asked by a student, "What makes a good leader?" I had a ready list, but I really didn't know. Line up ten people and ask them what made their leadership effective. There will be some crossovers—but most will admit they stumbled in the dark.

As you look across a graduating class, how able are you in assessing who will lead well in life? Or run your eye across a list of possible candidates for a position you're filling, and tell me who will succeed at the assignment and who won't. I've been wrong too often to feel much confidence in always getting it right.

Since university graduation in the mid-1960s, I've spent my time leading various ministries. At times I was lousy, and at others I think quite effective. And what made the difference? I don't know. What I've come to learn is that often the better moments are due to factors beyond our control. Other realities shape the time, and mitigating factors influence the opportunity. When I try really hard at being good at leading, at times I've tripped up, embarrassing myself and others. In moments when I forget about what I'm doing, it seems to work.

So what's the difference? Not knowing is not the same as being "un-smart" or unspiritual. Leadership, like painting, is an art. We learn various textures and characteristics of canvas, kinds of paint and technique. And then we practise, and practise, and practise.

Prayer—

Gracious God, who in all times and places knows why some things work out and others don't, help me hold loosely to what feels important for me to hold on to. For I know that when I'm at the point of defining what matters, in the light of Your appearance, it no longer does. So Father, may I not be caught up in trying to figure out why sometimes things work out and others don't, but may I rest in knowing that the Curator in time will explain. Amen.

Embracing Change

When Is the World Worldly?

"Greeks taught dualism: separating the spiritual from the material. The Church was trapped in this branching of life. It led to a class of priests who themselves were separated from the people. To Hebrews, this was strange: for them the mind and heart, belief and actions, weren't separated."

—*From my journal*

The dualism of my childhood church experience centred on the boogie word "worldliness." We knew what it was: for example, what went on in the back seats of cars—thank goodness most preachers forgot about or ignored our church hayrides!—and what women wore. We were so sure we had it right.

Our theology of spirituality had it partly right. Sincerity bathed our intensity in a certain holiness of heart that was hard to refute. Even so, it formed a pattern that created a false polarization between what was "of God" and what was "of the world."

As much as our focus on prayer, caring for neighbour, love of the church and living right had undeniable worth, this faulty world view separated part of God's world as if it didn't matter at all. No wonder the Evangelical world has in part grown up with a faulty view of Creation. If our inner person is really what Jesus came to save, the planet ends up not just second-best, but of little or no value. If serving God is best done as pastor, secular work is second-rate in the economy of God. You can see how the sacred-secular divide got replicated from music to vocation, from church to your calling, from Bible study to the arts.

Leaders have incredible influence in creating the lenses through which people see. I listen—occasionally—to popular TV preachers who are so self-assured about the diagrams they construct on how the world will end. People look at life as they're taught to see it. It's not only the words we use, but our strategies and methods that frame thinking, and by our influence those who take our leadership seriously come to think that way too.

Prayer—

God, You who exist beyond Creation and yet chose to live within, by Your Spirit keep breaking down those dividing walls that separate Your wider Creation and the life we live in this world. May the smugness of what I know become like dust beneath Your feet, so that as You mix spittle with that very dust, it'll bring healing of sight to those we love and serve. Amen.

Pushing the Boundaries

"Creative, leading-edge movements of the Church often have a touch of heresy and a smidge of cultism."

—From my journal

Heresy is what we view to be at variance with what we believe to be true. Cultism is the control (psychological) of a group by an idea or its leader. The two realities are common to the Christian Church.

Before we too quickly assume we can detect what is heresy and what is cultism, consider this question: What did the early Church first understand to be the importance of Peter's visit to Cornelius' home?

Peter, at first useless to the agenda of the Spirit in reaching beyond the Jewish community, had no heart to respond to the spiritual inquiry of this Roman, Cornelius. Peter first needed transformation (see Acts 10). Imagine him explaining to the disciples in Jerusalem why he went to minister to a Roman and his household. This pagan. This hated military presence.

Today we face shifts in culture and new expressions in the Church. Some of the post-modern "stuff" I like—some I don't. I'm careful not to too quickly dismiss their ideas and concerns. For I was raised in a Pentecostal world, a world many looked on as heretical and somewhat cultic. I have too sensitive a memory of having been dismissed out of hand to do the same to others.

Leaders are called on to take a longer view—to see within restless minds an authentic search for the Lord. It's too easy to fall into the trap of marginalizing one who might fall slightly outside your borders.

Prayer—

God of Truth, forever brooding over the "birds" of Your making, keep me from rejecting what I see to be the "ugly duckling" because he or she is different from me. Help me know that they too are Yours. In Your love and grace I offer this prayer. Amen.

When Not to Stand Still

"In business, the successful companies are not those that work at developing new products for their existing line, but those that aim at innovating new products for new business."

—Peter Drucker

I can see how this applies in commercial companies, but can it also work for caring vocations such as pastoring, counselling and social service work? Or is it an unfair layering of hard-nosed entrepreneurship over not-for-profit?

Drucker's genius is his ability to clue into the relentless forward movement of life, time and the universe as we age, grow and change. Let me go so far as to say his words have a familiar biblical ring. The Israelites, a few days out of Egypt, trapped by water in front and Egyptian troops behind, cried to Moses for help. His not surprising instruction was, "Stand still and see the hand of God" (Exodus 14).

The Lord retorted: "What in the world are you doing?"—my words—"Move on."

It was only in their walk of faith, pushing from here to there, that the Lord would be as they needed.

Leaders, we too get stuck. Faculty, the students you teach won't be the same tomorrow as they are today. Counsellors, your clients' hurts will be different tomorrow. Pastors, your congregation—that looks to you to lead—is living in a world of constant change. Helping others to see beyond now is an important part of our calling. The status quo disfigures and disables.

Wayne Gretzky, arguably the greatest of all hockey players, when asked of his prowess responded, "I never go where the puck is. I go to where it's going to be."

Prayer—

Timekeeper, the One who is never trapped in a moment, may there be a disquiet in my spirit that keeps me from being unwilling to move. Free me from platitudes of what I think You'll do, and instead may I hear Your voice calling so I too will lead as one willing to risk. Amen.

Watch Out from Behind

"In times of change, learners inherit the earth, while the learned find themselves beautifully equipped to deal with a world that no longer exists."

—*Eric Hoffer*

Hoffer, a longshoreman on the California docks with next to no formal education, spoke sanity into my generation of the '60s and '70s. He saw past the arrogance of many leaders of his day. He knew that learners have an attitude of humility: "There's so much more for me to know."

The "learned"—Hoffer speaks with tongue in cheek—really aren't learned. They just think they are. There are two kinds of learned leaders: those who are insecure but want their team to believe that they know it all, and those who don't know they don't know it all.

There were solid reasons for the radical movement of the 1960s. It wasn't just lazy, crazy students raising mischief. Rather they recognized an essential issue that needed correcting. In their eyes, the establishment had become arrogant. Inflexibility in organization, be it in private commerce or public institutions, had become entrenched. The world was changing, and leaders were either unwilling or too self-absorbed to notice.

I hear the unease some of my contemporaries have with the emerging Church. Here's a warning to church leaders: We have much yet to learn about the ways of God with His people. In each generation, the Spirit is creative, speaking by way of the language and culture of the day. For us of former generations, recognize that even as the Spirit spoke to our generation, He will speak to this and coming generations in language they best understand.

We know death is inevitable, yet we choose to ignore it. So too we know that it's inevitable that change is recurring, yet we ignore it. Locked into patterns of worship, paradigms of congregational life or ways of seeing the world, we assume by age and experience that we're learned. Even so, the Spirit continues to raise up new generations of learners who'll bring transitions and changes. For those of us who think we're the learned, step aside and allow the learners to help us inherit the earth.

Prayer—

God of each generation—Abraham, Isaac and Jacob—keep me from trying to serve a need that no longer exists. May humility infuse my heart, so that in learning I'll understand You ride alongside each generation in its day and with its forms. As I pass on to others the best I know, may it be humility that carries whatever I think I know, so my life will show others that I'm ever learning, as did Mary, the mother of Jesus, seeking to understand. Amen.

The Price of Tuition

"Once you've figured out what you want to do, find someone who has done it before...If they share your values and aspirations, and if they freely share their counsel, they can help you through rough patches and celebrate your victories as their own."

—Howard Schultz, Starbucks CEO

I frankly don't know if it's because I mirror my generation—I was born in 1942—or because I typify a personality type, but my first inclination wasn't to find another who had "done it before." Yes, I had my heroes. There were a few that if I could have been like them, I would have. Fact is, with one I tried really hard. And it was here I got it wrong.

I mixed up learning from another who was doing what I wanted to do with trying to do it the same way. Was I insecure about not doing it my way? Or did I misunderstand the role of modelling? I'm not sure. In the end, after an embarrassing failure, I began to look to the substance of his work and not the method of his delivery. His name was Jay Kessler. He was in senior leadership in youth ministry in the States, as I was in Canada.

My life and understanding of ministry had been nurtured in a revivalist world. The youth counterculture of the '60s and '70s didn't make sense of the noise or language of my religious tribe. They had another dialect and operated at higher decibels.

If ever I've envied, it was then. His skills in communication were what I wanted to emulate. He gave me time. He travelled north from Wheaton to spend time with me, and I travelled south to his place. He didn't teach me his way of speaking—he helped me learn to understand.

What a gift. I learned to feel comfortable in my own sneakers, while always being stretched to see beyond the obvious to learn what was beneath. Jay taught me "back door" thinking. While everyone was charging through the front door on issues, he led me to discover insights from another perspective. And by watching and listening, I learned from him how to speak about matters of faith in language other than heavy religious chatter.

A gift beyond the price of tuition.

Prayer—

Faithful Friend, Master Pedagogue, how tenderly You help us see that it's our gifts You wish us to exercise, not pressing us to excel in mimicry. Indeed, we blossom as our gifting absorbs wisdom and counsel from others, and then mixed by the exuberance of Your indwelling Spirit, we slowly emerge in doing what we do best. How gracious You are. Amen.

A Beneficial Rain

"When handed a lemon, make lemonade."

—*Public wisdom*

Catchy sayings often seem trivial at best. But lest I lose a good idea by inbred cynicism, note the wise words of this leader.

It was amidst the media hubbub during the release of *The Da Vinci Code* movie. The group getting blasted by this disingenuous novel was Opus Dei, literally meaning "the work of God."

Note how they handled a misaligned and slanderous attack. Author Dan Brown depicted them as a disreputable, devious cult lurking in the shadows of the Vatican. Instead of crying victim, they invited the press to better understand them.

They followed the wise words of their founder, St. Josemaría Escrivá: "The evil or flippant word of only one man can create a climate of opinion, and even make it fashionable to speak badly about somebody. Then that thin mist of slander rises from below, reaches a high level and perhaps condenses into black clouds. But when the man persecuted in this way is a soul of God, the clouds shower down a beneficial rain, come what may; and the Lord ensures that He is exalted by the very means with which they tried to humiliate or defame Him."

Now that's leadership.

Inclined to fix a problem, right a wrong or correct a misunderstanding, I plunge into the underbrush, trying to defend. When it comes from unfair criticism, I rehearse the arguments that seem so convincing and persuasive, waiting for the right moment or pressing to create the moment myself.

Billy Graham had a motto: "No response to criticism."

Criticism, fair or unfair, can be of benefit. It can be turned into a "beneficial rain."

Prayer—

God of All-knowing, whatever is hidden in the criticism of this day, be it slanderous or fair, false or accurate, guard my spirit from a defensive posture. Instead, help me seek to let Your light shine, so Your life is the resulting reality. Amen.

Calling It Quits

"It is not the critic who counts."

—*Theodore Roosevelt*

Wander through Westminster Abbey and observe its many tombs and inscriptions. Then walk through a city park, by a cenotaph, and note to whom the plaques and sculptures are dedicated—not to book reviewers, political pundits, art critics or detractors of any kind. They're written and erected to those who did something for humankind.

This isn't a defence against critics. Leaders need them. Critics help to keep us facing issues. They call us to higher standards. They remind us that we can't get away with what others can. For if we do, the consequences are too severe.

Rather I want to encourage you to not be unduly depleted by the constant and unrelenting criticism you may be facing this week. When you feel like throwing in the towel because a small mistake has been blown out of proportion, reign in your feelings of self-pity and remind yourself that to lead is your calling.

Roosevelt said it well:

> *It is not the critic who counts; not the man who points out how the strong man stumbles, or where the doers of deeds could have done them better. The credit belongs to the man who is actually in the arena, whose face is marred by dust and sweat and blood; who strives valiantly; who errs, and comes short again and again because there is no effort without error and shortcomings; but who does actually strive to do the deeds; who knows the great enthusiasms, the great devotions; who spends himself in worthy cause; who at the best knows in the end triumph of high achievement, and who at the worst, if he fails, at least fails while daring greatly, so that his place shall never be with those cold and timid souls who know neither victory nor defeat.*

Prayer—

Crucified One of Calvary, You who were shackled by Your own creation, keep me from wanting to call it quits when unfairness overtakes. Your Spirit refusing to camouflage my errors instead fills me with strength so I can keep on doing, even in my fallenness, that which is good. Forgive me. Cleanse my duplicitous heart. Strengthen my weak knees. Give surety to my unsure hands. By Your grace, I won't stop because either fairly or unfairly I've been criticized. I'll go on in Your strong Name. Amen.

Gifting to Lead

Real Wranglers Wanted

"A person who has had a bull by the tail once has learned sixty or seventy times as much as a person who hasn't."

—*Mark Twain*

I've been in some form of leadership for over 40 years. After completing studies at the University of Toronto in the mid-1960s, I began my life in leadership, and the business of leading hasn't stopped. I wish I'd been smarter sooner. I've made some mistakes along the way. I've done a few things right. But nothing seems to get me down more than making a wrong hire, especially when I have no one to thank but myself.

As a leader, I'm always looking for people to lead. I'm an optimist: "Oh, you want to do it, and yes, I see you've got arms so...yes, you'll do." I'm too easily taken in by someone who wants to do the job. Passion sells me every time—but sometimes it doesn't work out.

Mark Twain got it right. When your job is herding cattle, and it's up to you to hire wranglers, make sure you hire someone who has been pulled along, holding on to the tail of a beast of the field. I've come to learn that it's better for everyone involved to hire someone who has wrestled cattle to the ground than hire a wannabe wrangler who has only sat on the sidelines, watching.

I love the relationship Moses had with young Joshua. Before the younger took over managing the Hebrews in their wanderings, Moses had him go through his paces (Exodus 24:13).

There's something about experience that becomes an important litmus test.

Prayer—

Loving Friend, Holy Presence, help me live within the tension of being optimistic about those willing to serve, and yet diligent to carefully raise up leaders who want to learn and are willing to be mentored. May the example of Moses compel me to encourage new leadership, while at the same time making a conscious effort to equip them. So that in the end, our enterprises will take on the "Jordans" of life, leading people into the land promised. Amen.

Moving from Comfort Zones

"You must at some point take a 'leap of faith' toward the emerging model of what it means to truly lead, and away from the need to be successful, famous, rich, in control, or powerful. The kind of leadership I am advocating is out of the understanding of pain, the loss of innocence, the love of others, the larger purpose, the pursuit of wisdom, the honor of life. Ask yourself if you are willing to take the risk."

—*J. Hagberg in* Real Power: Stages of Personal Power in Organizations

Now that I'm older, I see more clearly the mistakes I've made in leadership and ministry. On occasion, I wake up in the middle of the night and think of a mistaken judgment or inappropriate comment, and cringe.

In the morning, it seems less serious. (I've learned never to believe what I see by the flickering candle of night until it's seen in the brightness of day.) What changes in the daylight is that I see mistakes as part of the collateral of moving forward.

Not to justify stupidity, carnality or self-centredness, leading requires risk-taking. Abraham left his family all because he heard a Voice calling. That risk changed history, bringing into humankind a people whose race has influenced civilizations. Many factors characterize leadership, but none like risk-taking. There are times when that hurts others, but if we never move beyond secure boundaries, benefits that might accrue, won't.

If you note the text (Genesis 12 and 13), at the same time Abraham was called on to risk, he moved out from the securities and knowns of his home. He was uprooted. He moved from what was familiar into uncharted territory.

There's a familiar ring to that line. I've found that to risk, I need to let go of the comfort of what I know, and step into a world where only with His help will I succeed or even survive. My hunch is that the two go together. Achieving involves risk. Risk requires new places, people, ideas and resources.

Prayer—

Father of Creation and Lord of Invention, may Your Spirit help me overcome my impulse to protect reputation and earnings with an unfaith-like caution. My leap of faith isn't in the dark, but in the full light of Your being here, today, in this place. For that, I give You praise. Amen.

Surprised

"Every time I move out of my comfort zone, the Lord expands my world."

—*From my journal*

The CBC (the Canadian government-sponsored national broadcaster) dealt with the death of Jerry Falwell citing his most reprehensible anti-gay comments. There was nothing redeeming—so construed the CBC—in his life.

I was no fan of Falwell. Some of his comments seemed pompous and harsh, as far from Jesus as I could imagine. He was embarrassing, and seldom showed humility. However, that he was faithful to parts and elements of the Gospel is evident, and he built an impressive university.

My life intersected with his in the early 1980s. In 1980, Ronald Reagan had won the White House, helped by Jerry Falwell and his Moral Majority leaving behind his fellow Evangelical, Jimmy Carter.

During the lead-up to the election we—on the north side of the 49th parallel—became increasingly uncomfortable with Falwell's analysis and prescriptions. It was simply that Canadians sometimes see issues differently than Americans. Further, he had his strong support in the highly religious southern US—his comments may have seemed okay there. But from where I sat, too often they undercut our witness of Christ.

I was asked by a friend why it was that Falwell seemed to get so much air time in Canada. Before he finished asking the question, I knew the answer. In silence, whoever speaks first is heard. We hadn't cultivated in Canada a voice for Evangelicals.

In responding (or maybe reacting) to Falwell, I discovered something new and life-changing. Falwell pressed Canadians—and I suspect Americans as well—to engage in debates, to provide alternative views and solutions to engender a more balanced conversation instead of a rant.

Looking back over these decades of leadership, I didn't do what I'd planned. Instead, I responded to a life reality, and in that response discovered the leading of the Spirit in places and ways I never could've imagined.

Prayer—

Holy Spirit, God behind, God in front, God around, ever present and always knowing, may I not be so concerned about achieving a goal as to feel Your nudge. Planning is so correct. It seems assuring, but it exposes my need for security in my plans and not a trust in Your leading. I wish not to absolve myself from the discipline of good planning, but please help my spirit find opportunities in new discoveries opened by Your hand. Amen.

Failure Opens Doors

"Successful careers are not planned. They develop when people are prepared for opportunities because they know their strengths, their method of work, and their values."

—Peter Drucker

If you're over 50, cast your eye over your life and career. Could you have ever anticipated back in your earlier days where you'd be now? Colleague Don Posterski noted, "Life is not a straight line from A to Z; it's a zigzag."

I started out flushed with anticipation that our church group and I from the onset would break out in society-altering ways: frankly, not a bad way to begin. "Better to control the fire than to have to re-ignite it." The vision wasn't misguided or inappropriate—just somewhat naïve.

Year by year, and experience by experience, I accumulated ideas critical to action and self-awareness. These—without much outside interference or nudging—have a way of sorting out the next step, the next place, the next initiative.

And surprise after surprise. What I thought I'd be and believed to be most significant, didn't materialize. What I expected to be, didn't happen. I still have memories of feeling deeply disappointed about what I so wanted to become.

Drucker's insight fits. Careers are more defined by opportunities in times and places that we least expect. While trying to follow my boyhood dream to be an evangelist, Lily and I were walking the country roads outside a southern Manitoba Mennonite village, wondering what had gone wrong. It was then a letter came from Youth for Christ in Montreal. Though my father advised me to say "no," a pastor and mentor, Dr. Harry Faught, said, "This may be right for you." It was. That opportunity shifted my life. What it did more poignantly was open up an understanding of gifts and strengths—in areas I had no clue of gifting.

My advice? Look for opportunities. They may not match what you think your gifts are, or even what you know they are. But those open doors will move you into greater self-awareness, refining your essential giftings, and pressing you beyond your comfort zone to rely on the Spirit in ways you never would have without taking the risk.

Prayer—

Great Lord and Spirit, who inspired the psalmist to help us know that in trusting You, You'll direct our paths, help me see doors that are slightly ajar, which if pushed open, would make available corridors of opportunities of Your doing. Give me, Lord, discernment to make a choice, and boldness to move when the time comes. Amen.

Overcoming Resistance

"Leading and driving a car have two indisputable things in common: both must overcome resistance to moving forward."

—*Peter Koestenbaum*

Psychodynamic

Koestenbaum, in pointing out three dynamics that lead to resistance, begins with the psychodynamic. Any group embodies a variety of psychological dynamics: an adult angry over how they were treated by a parent, most often the father; others not having matured become insolent and sulk if they don't get their own way. I met a person who, though very experienced in leading an institution, behaved in a passive/aggressive manner. At one moment he was compliant, understanding and helpful, and then without warning would launch into an attack, bizarre and over the top. So it goes.

These are life experiences that inflict on people their hangovers of debilitating experiences and memories, and may cause them to shut down their willingness to work and co-operate with others. While a leader is not called to act as psychologist to staff and other members, even just understanding those lingering realities will free you from personal recrimination and self-doubt.

Systemic

Systems can get stuck. People often prefer and resort to the status quo, of the opinion that what they're doing is good for everyone. People, inwardly focused, unaware of how they're seen and quite unaware of what else exists—besides their point of view—inhabit every organization.

Systems get locked in when people, tripped up by a desire to be measured by political correctness, pull any lever available to stop new thinking from having a say. While the term "thinking outside the box" is overused, it's a helpful picture to see what needs doing.

Existential

For those fearful of another idea being of more value or even truer than theirs, anxiety sets in. Fuelled by insecurity, their feelings can pressure the organization to a protective but isolated stance, out of touch and lacking awareness of what else may be.

In dealing with broken walls of organizations, at the heart of the need is change or, more precisely, conversion. Tinkering with its purpose and structure may not be sufficient. Bringing in a new idea may not in itself help bring a turnaround. The biblical term is *metanoia*—literally meaning a new birth, or birth from above.

Prayer—

Lord of the New, in managing this enterprise may I be a channel of Your life-changing presence. Keep me from overpowering others with my hope for a quick change, and instead be patient, ever working with You, God's Spirit, in bringing needed change. Amen.

Lessons on Resistance

"Leadership is taking the way of least resistance."

—*Bob Cooley*

When I heard this, I asked Bob if I'd heard him right. As mentor and former seminary president, I took seriously what he had to say.

Rugged, take-no-prisoners leadership is the myth of my childhood. In watching the US presidential primaries, political pundits took note of what they saw as toughness of the young senator-wanting-to-be-president as he took a swipe at his opponent. "Now that's leadership!" could be heard echoing from homes across America.

It's taken me time to learn the importance of Bob's line. This isn't all there is to this subject, but it's important. Resistance comes from a variety of sources. It may be something that needs to be overcome for the sake of the mission. It could be factors that thwart the idea of the call and need to be defeated or pushed aside. People, policies or programs may conspire in a rather deliberate way to defeat the idea, but only occasionally.

Coming into an academic world posed new challenges. It's a world where process rules, and whatever you planned to do, double the time you think it requires. I was asked how I worked in an academic community, assuming faculties usually objected to new ideas. Yes, new ideas might upset their rather conservative nature. However, I learned that when an idea was materially resisted, it was because the idea was flawed, it needed more refinement, or it was good but the timing was wrong.

In each case, it pushes leadership back to the drawing board.

As a leader, I don't like to be opposed. Ego pushes up my back. Impatience snaps a retort. Hurt feelings pick up marbles and walk away. Sometimes the best response is "no." We're well served when flaws are flagged.

Taking the way of least resistance isn't because I want to get along.

It's not that I'm forfeiting leadership or bowing to please others. Rather it's because there may be a better way or time.

I've learned the hard way that resistance can be my friend.

Prayer—

Creator of Personality and Spirit of Guidance, whose agenda is Kingdom-good, may grace, patience and self-giving govern, so the goals are never abridged, motives never sullied and communities never diminished. This is Your work. May we do what You have in mind, and in Your time. Amen.

CASTLE QUAY BOOKS